DRAGONS

and

TIGERS

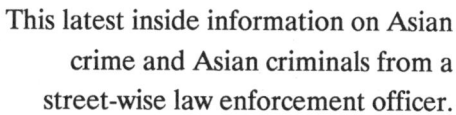

This latest inside information on Asian crime and Asian criminals from a street-wise law enforcement officer.

Timely, factual, and helpful, this books provides tips and tested procedures for bridging the cultural gaps between western justice systems and the refugees from Vietnam, Laos, China, Japan, Korea, Cambodia and other Asian countries.

JAMES R. BADEY

DRAGONS and TIGERS

James R. Badey

Copyright (c) by James R. Badey, 1988

International Standard Book Number
0-912479-05-1

PALMER ENTERPRISES
P.O. Box 1714
Loomis, California
95650

With love to my mother, who always said she would write a book if only she could spell.

Preface

There exists a history and tradition of organized criminal activity in the Asian countries of Vietnam, China, Japan, and Korea. Peoples from these countries are immigrating and travelling throughout the free world in larger numbers than ever before. The majority of these immigrants and travellers have proven to be honest and law abiding productive citizens who have resettled only to better their lives. The small number of criminals among them, however, will also have the opportunities to better their lives, increase their standards of living, all the while becoming more proficient in their criminal endeavors. The free societies that have accepted them are proving to be fertile grounds for these career criminals.

It is incumbent upon all law enforcement officers and administrators to become educated in the languages and cultures of these new citizens in order to be effective in dealing with their unique crime problems and other needs. Only after a high level of awareness has been developed and practiced will law enforcement be able to make intelligent requests for resources from the U.S. Congress and from the various state and local governments.

When the author first began work in his particular Asian community, there was no single text or 'how to' resource to which he could turn in order to clarify the overall Asian crime picture. With this handbook he has attempted to fill that void so that the men and women in other law enforcement agencies with similar assignments to his may have a reasonable point from which to depart.

The PUBLISHER

Contents

DRAGONS and TIGERS

Acknowledgements

No book has ever been written without assistance of one sort or another. This handbook is no exception. There are many friends and acquaintances both in my profession of law enforcement and outside of it who contributed considerably in material, time, effort, and other support. DRAGONS and TIGERS is truly the end product of the efforts of many people.

Special thanks are due to Chief William K. Stover and retired Deputy Chief William E. Packett, Arlington County Police Department, Virginia. Without their insight, foresight, and continued support, I would never have had the opportunity to devote my police work for the betterment of Asian citizens in our community.

A special debt will always be owed to Detective Robert Y.R. Chung of the New York City Police Department - - a real professional and a most honorable man whom I am honored to call my 'younger brother.' Many others, such as; Bobby Lum and the Asian module of the New York City Police Department's Intelligence Unit; Kathy Johnston and Homer Moy, Boston Police Department; Bill Gatter, Philadelphia Police Department; Jack Willoughby, New Orleans Police Department; Jerry Ellis, Houston Police Department; Bob Casey, formerly with Houston and now with the Federal Bureau of Investigation; John McKenna, (Retired), San Francisco Police Department; Doug Zwemke, San Jose Police Department; Dan Lyons, Garden Grove Police Department; Don Saviers, Westminster Police Department; Glenn Furakawa, Honolulu Police Department; George Cowley, Metropolitan Toronto Police Force, Canada; and Fred Wong and Al Miyashiro of the Federal Bureau of Investigation who encouraged me throughout my writing.

I would be remiss if I did not thank my sometimes partner, Mike Rudy, and the other Arlington officers and police officers throughout the world, too numerous to list, who assisted and inspired me in this work.

Mr. Charles R. Sheehan receives total credit for the chapter on language and cross-cultural communication. Mr. Sheehan is retired from the Foreign Service Institute, U.S. Department of State. He is a respected linquist with almost 30 years of experience in Asian languages.

I will always be grateful to my publisher who recognized the need for this book and who initiated its undertaking. And to Cindy Dimmock who did the final preparations for delivery of the words and pictures to the publisher. And, of course, to my son, Mike, who contributed design ideas for the book's cover.

A special and most heartfelt thanks is rendered to my wife, Reta, and to our children, Paul and Jaime. Their many sacrifices made in order to allow me the time and freedom to do my research and writing were greatly appreciated.

JRB

CHAPTER ONE

From Los Angeles, U.S.A., to Toronto, Canada, and Sydney, Australia, newspaper headlines scream out at their readers such things as:

"ASIAN GANGS PLAGUE CITIES,"
and
"GANGS FIGHT VIET CONFLICT OF A DIFFERENT SORT."

These headlines and others like them are more often than not followed by factual and well written stories. However, the fact remains the reported incidents are isolated and out of context to the full spectrum of the true situation in the new Asian homelands of Australia, Canada, the United States, and elsewhere.

1. Vietnamese

When we look at the Vietnamese in the latter half of the 1980's, we must also look back to their beginning in the 20th Century for the full meaning behind their current state of affairs. The French government, which came to Vietnam in the early 1900's, came as a strong military power and was there simply for economic reasons. They were the true colonialists who acted as though Vietnam existed for France's benefit alone. The political and economic situation grew worse over the years that followed. This gave great impetus to a nationalistic movement along with other political ideologies which attempted to assert their way of life upon that country's historically exploited masses.

French colonialism, Japanese occupation, the French-Indochina war, and more recently the long war involvement with the United States and other nations contributed nothing positive in the form of political leadership for the newly established government of South Vietnam in the mid-1950's. Public office was not sought for idealistic political reasons but for personal gain and power. Corruption quickly became an established way of life and profiteering became a profession.

By 1955, the two powerful political-religious sects, Hoa Hao and Cao Dai, had joined the criminal organization, Binh Xuyen. The Binh Xuyen controlled the Saigon-Cholon Police and Security Services. They also controlled the countrys gambling and prostitution from which they made huge profits. Portions of these profits were shared with the various heads of Vietnam's government. From this sharing of profits was formed a coalition of power which posed a real threat to any attempt at building a stable goverment. This unlikely joining together of the religious sects and organized crime elements produced nothing other than a growing number of political gangsters who systematically plundered their nation's resources.

By October, 1955, the government of South Vietnam successfully completed their campaign of eradicating the influence and power of the religious sects and the Binh Xuyen. The few Binh Xuyen members who survived the battle were dispersed to the countryside. The next twenty years were no better economically and politically than had been the years before 1955. Corruption was still a way of life and profiteering was still very much a profession.(1)

The elimination of the Binh Xuyen in 1955 did not eliminate the activities of gambling, prostitution, and opium dealing from the country. Now, in the place of the Binh Xuyen gangsters, there were many high ranking government officials and military officers who filled the void by supplying and controlling these activities.

Black marketing and profiteering were the primary ways to make a lucrative living during the years following 1955. Legislators routinely sold their votes to the highest bidders and exemptions from military service were easily purchased by anyone possessing the required amount of money. The corruption of the leaders at all levels throughout the country rendered the government weak and ineffective.

2. Waves of Immigrants

History shows the government of South Vietnam collapsed in 1975 followed immediately by a great exodus of its people to America and elsewhere in the free world. The first wave of Vietnamese immigrants came as a result of the fall of Saigon in April, 1975. For the most part, these people generally had some connection with the collapsed government and with the military forces of the United States. However, a large number of the corrupt government and military officers made it into the lines of the evacuees as did many of the private business people who had been profiteering for years from the black market.

The thousands of immigrants scattered to many countries including the United States, Canada, England, France, Germany, and Australia. The criminals among the immigrant population had sufficient time to establish themselves in their new communities during the four years immediately following the first exodus and before the second exodus occurred. By the time the second exodus began and the masses of boat people had arrived in their new countries, the first wave of immigrants were solidly based in positions of influence and were busy developing additional power bases from which to operate.

3. The Boat People

The Vietnamese boat people have been the topic of many news stories and public discussions. They have been depicted as desperate heroes escaping poverty and totalitarianism of the Socialist Republic of Vietnam. Frequently there are emotional stories, written by the press, about refugee families who have become established and are already climbing the ladder to success.(2) Because of these reports, these recent arrivals have been welcomed with open arms by the people of the United States and elsewhere in the free world.

However, there is another side to some of these so-called success stories. It involves a large share of the immigrant population, their criminal backgrounds, and their willingness to participate in crime even in their new homelands.

What does the reader say to the statement, "About 20 to 30 percent of the boat people are not escapees from the political upheaval." These are the constant figures provided by Vietnamese immigrants. If these 20 to 30 percent are not escapees, who are they? According to consistent information, this figure represents three groups of people who have left Vietnam.

0   Government throw-aways
0   Criminals
0   Trained espionage agents

The first category, government throw-aways, was and is made up of non-productive citizens who the new Socialist Republic of Vietnam government felt stood little chance of ever becoming productive under their regime. To some extent, this group is made up of persons the government feels cannot be rehabilitated to their way of thinking. This group also includes the misfits, the malcontents, and known trouble makers.

The second group, criminals, consists of petty, minor, and mid-level but successful criminals. These typically include the pimps, prostitutes, gamblers, and minor drug dealers.

The third group is <u>espionage agents</u>. These may be either trained profession-als, those who have been brainwashed or turned around, or just plain simple folks who are being exploited through their ties with family members who reside in Vietnam. These spies do what is required of them not for any great monetary rewards but for reasons of duty, honor, and promises of assistance for their family members still in Vietnam. The motivation of these spies is irrelevant. Their potential and actual accomplishments should be our concern. These spies are every bit as dangerous and disruptive as any criminal street gang or criminal enterprise.

4. Chinese

Exhibit 1 - Triad Symbol

When the topic turns to Chinese organized crime in the American law enforcement community, the terms "Triad" and "Tong" are often interchanged in the belief they are one and the same. This is not the case. It is essential for law enforcement practitio-ners to understand the difference and to articulate that understanding. To use the two terms incorrectly merely emphasizes a lack of awareness and broadens the credibility gap between the Chinese Community and law enforcement. The term, "Triad", is not an English translation of any Chinese word or symbol. It is simply an English term given to describe the emblem of the Chinese secret societies. This emblem is a triangle with the sides representing the three powers of heaven, earth, and man.(3)

Chinese living in Hong Kong refer to the Triad Society in several ways:(4)

0	Sam Hop Wui	(Three United Association)
0	Tin Tei Wui	(Heaven and Earth Association)
0	Hung Mun	(Hung Sect) or

0   Hak Sh'e Wui   (Black Society Association)

This last name, Hak Sh'e Wui, is of comparitively recent origin and reflects present day public opinion the Society is something sinister and evil rather than a mystic brotherhood of man.(5)

In its original form, the Triad Society was comprised of five lodges which covered the whole of China. It was the Triad's Second Lodge which covered the Kwang/Kwangsi area, including the city of Canton, and from which the majority of worldwide Chinese soceiities originate. This lodge has the most impact on the people of Hong Kong.

In its earliest phases, the Triad Society was a Chinese secret organization whose members, each bound by oaths of blood brotherhood, were pledged to overthrow the foreign conquerors of their country and to restore the ancient ruling house of Ming to the throne of China.

In a highly dated book by author Harold Irwin Cleveland of the Chicago Times-Herald, he wrote extensively about a network of secret societies in old China. His book is cited here to further demonstrate that the Triads were a dynamic force in China long before the turn of this century. The following are direct quotes from his book, Massacres of Christians by Heathen Chinese.(6)

"A Chinaman appears to be well contented with himself when he is a member of at least one secret society and with ample opportunity to become a member of a dozen or more, should he need them in the future. The (Chinese) Empire is a network in its social life of secret societies. Every need of life in the Empire appears to be met by the people with an organization or a secret society to overcome that need. The struggle for existence is something frightful. It is almost impossible for the ordinary subject to ever reach the ears of the Emperor or his councillors with a complaint. Yet aid is needed and the Chinese mind, quick to invent substitute for the Imperial authority, has selected the secret society as its medium for securing redress or needed help."

"Even beggars have their societies with their statutes, special code, feasts, and gatherings," Cleveland reported from his observations of China.

"The purpose of many of these societies is pure, and without them it is impossible to think of anything but chaos reigning in a large number of the settlements of the Empire. But others which started with a pure purpose have degenerated and come under the influence of strong men with vicious dispositions. This has led, in numerous instances, to murder being advocated and into practice where the purpose of a society has been thwarted by some outside human agency."

"The Triad Secret Society," Cleveland noted, "is the oldest and most famous of the many Chinese organizations of a similar character. Its origin is so remote that the society's book of rites contains the statement that it existed "since the foundation of the earth." The real name of the league is T'ien-Ti Hwey, or Hung League; the name 'Triad' comes from "Sam-Hop Hwey," the popular title given to the organization. The society's teachings are exaulted, to such a degree, that many of them seem to come bodily out of the Sermon on the Mount. Unfortunately, however, their practice is different from their teaching. A more cruel organization was never created to become a thorn in the flesh of all workers in the cause of law and order."

Throughout the history of China there is evidence of the existence of secret societies; however, the Triad Society as it is known today is generally accepted as having been first established in the 17th Century. From the beginning, the Triad Society strongly adhered to the code of secrecy and continued to believe secrecy was of paramount importance towards the success of their operations. They also relied upon fear to neutralize public and government actions by making it known that all who opposed them faced certain death. Contributing also to the solidifying cohesiveness of their society were their mystic initiation rites and blood oaths of brotherhood.(7)

Some have said that new rulers of China often acquired their positions with the direct help of the Triads. As a result, many rulers added to the power of the Triads by extending to them their personal support and protection. Once they were in position to enjoy the goodwill of the ruler they dropped their purely political objectives and focused upon their ever growing strength and organization. They then were free to devise methods to reach their financial goals. Their machinations were overlooked and given tacit approval by their indebted rulers.

5. Escape to Hong Kong

By 1857, many believed the societies had gained control of the Chinese labor market. The ruler found this not to his liking and dispatched his imperial troops to round them up in order to bring the power of the societies to a halt. Between 1857 and 1912, waves of Triad members fled the country by crossing the border at Hong Kong. They set up new branches of the old Triad Society as soon as they arrived. Their arrival did not escape the notice of the British police. In 1885, the Captain Superintendent of Police for the Crown Colony stated: ". . . it would appear that all the lower criminal classes of the Colony have joined the Triad Society and look to the heads of it for assistance when they are arrested."(8)

By 1900, these old secret societies, for most practical purposes, were no longer political action groups but merely criminal cartels involved in opium smuggling, prostitution, protection rackets, and other crimes. The 'Society watchers' could find no other purpose for their existence.

In 1949, when the Nationalists were defeated by the Communists, the defeated armies and pro Nationalist people took refuge in Hong Kong, Taiwan, and elsewhere. These refugees from mainland China brought with them their secret societies. The Triad associations were the common denominator for many of these immigrants.

Currently, the Triad Societies remain criminally active in Hong Kong. No society has a monopoly on any particular form of criminal enterprise and there is no "Godfather" image in the overall Triad movement. The official posture of law enforcement in Hong Kong is the Triad Societies are a major threat to law and order.(9)

Police authorities in the Colony report they have no evidence to show any one Triad leader within their jurisdiction can exert leadership over any criminal activity outside of the Colony. The single exception would be through some crime syndicate involved in smuggling between Hong Kong and some overseas location.(10)

There are documented reports which establish the existence of a major Triad in Taiwan which has expanded its operation to Hong Kong. These same documents show they seek further expansion in Chinese communities throughout the world.(11) This documentation, along with testimony given to the President's Commission on Organized Crime, demonstrates Triads do exist outside of Hong Kong thus making them international in scope.

The above research leads to the conclusion that Triad Societies are not the altruistic secret societies of Chinese myth and legend but merely organized criminal cartels of Asian origin. This conclusion is not the author's alone. Fenton Bresler, in his statement to the President's Commission on Organized Crime, said, "My considered judgment worked out over two years of active research is that there are two basic kinds of criminal Triad activity in operation throughout the world. Both stem from the teeming cities of the Far East, the forging ground of Triad membership. Both operate on the basis of an ethnic Chinese network which gives criminals, through their shared Triad membership, availability to an underground of international criminal activity."

"This first kind of basic activity is more loosely organized and is typified by the street gangs of Hong Kong or the youth gangs in the United States. Its members may not call themselves Triads even though their secret societies follow Triad traditions, structures, and methods."

"The second basic pattern of criminal activity is more fearsome. It is, I'm fairly convinced, an organized international conspiracy with a strict hierarchy operating from flexible control over its members and with an almost limitless capacity for criminal evil stretching across the world."(12) Most law enforcement officials, experienced in Asian Crime, firmly believe the Triads are nothing more than organized criminal enterprises.

6. The Tong Organization

The English word 'Tong' has its roots in the Chinese word 'Tang'. Tang is the Chinese term for the English word 'party'. In 1610, a group of political reformers were referred to as a 'Tang'; that is, an organized clique subversive to both imperial authority and the current bureaucratic process. Many Chinese immigrated to the United States during the mid-nineteenth century. They thought of America as "The land of the golden mountain." Their dreams were to come to this country to work in the mines. The majority of them arrived as poor, single men who had no friends in the new homelands. They found themselves alone and strangers in an inhospitable land. Soon they joined Chinese working groups that formed up along the lines of their labor. There were laundry Tongs, medicine Tongs, and many others based on work and even on places of birth. Nothing was mysterious or sinister about the Tongs and joining a Tong meant the members were part of a friendly and fraternal association where they could seek protection and guidance.

From these initial loosely knit fraternal and social organizations the Tongs slowly began to develop into organizations with a structured leadership. With structure, leadership, and increased membership, the Tongs changed course slightly. They became involved in their own de facto governments where they decided issues, resolved disputes, and acted as a quasi control body over many of the Chinese in America.

By the 1880's, the Tongs began to call themselves Benevolent Associations. A critical point, to be noted at this time, is that membership in the Tongs was always limited to persons of Chinese descent. Through limiting membership in this manner, the conversion to the Benevolent Associations went little noted by the non-Chinese in the communities. When their strength was finally acknowledged by non-Chinese, the Tongs were already strongly structured and in place.

Contrary to the unanimous agreement of law enforcement to the principal and fact that Triads are organized criminal enterprises, there is no such consensus of opinion regarding the goals of Chinese Tongs. It may be said the Tongs are still in an evolutionary process. The process began with the good and wholesome objectives of fraternalism and group support. But it is apparent, as they have grown, that these goals have become tarnished in varying degrees. Leadership, in some instances, has been taken over by criminals with Triad connections and is continually being infiltrated by the criminal element of the community. The definitive link between certain Chinese street gangs and certain Tongs has been documented.(13) These factors, coupled with the geo-political situation in Hong Kong and the ever increasing scope of the Triad influence present all of law enforcement with a formidable challenge.

7.   Japanese Boryokudan

The Japanese National Police call their organized crime factions Boryokudan which literally translates in English as "violent ones." Elsewhere in the world, they are known as "Yakuza." The term Yakuza was first used by gamblers in 17th century Japan.   According to the most widely held belief, the term derives from the worst possible score in the card game called "hanafuda" or flower cards.   This game is played with three cards being dealt to each player in the game and the last digit total counts as the number in the hand. A hand of 20 - - the worst possible score - - gives the holder a total of zero.(14)   Among the losing combinations, a sequence of 8-9-3 in Japanese translates to Ya-ku-sa.   The term Yakuza was used widely by Japanese gamblers themselves to denote something useless. They later applied it to mean they

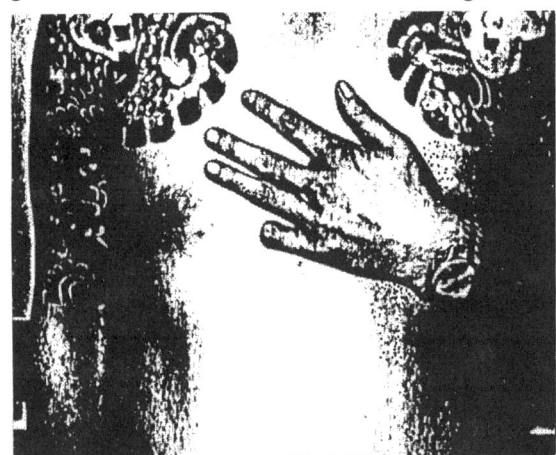

were useless to society and were born to lose.   Its use has been expanded by the general public in Japan to cover all organized crime groups of Japanese origin.(15)

Yakuza or Boryokudan are widely known for two physical characteristics which place them apart from the general citizenry. These are: Amputated finger digits (*Yubisume*) and elaborate body tattoos.(16)(17)

Exhibit 2 - Amputated Little Finger

8.   Price Paid for Error

The custom of Yubisume in which the top joint of the little finger is severed is practised by the Yakuza.   The errant follower ceremoniously cuts off the top digit of his little finger, wraps it in white cloth, and presents it to his boss. The boss accepts it, puts it in a jar, and places the jar alongside jars containing the digits received from other errant followers. The individual cutting off his finger is acknowledging his error and asking forgiveness. It is not uncommon for errant followers to be forgiven more than once and thus add to the boss's collection of finger digits. By accepting the finger, the boss demonstrates his granting of forgiveness. Today, this ceremony is still practiced, however, it is done in a hospital setting utilizing modern safeguards.

9. Body Decorations

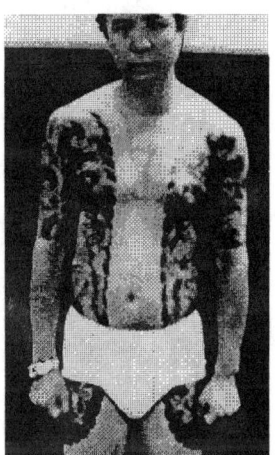

Tattooing has a long history in Japan. Originally, even before feudal times, Japanese criminals were tattooed with black rings around their arms for each offense committed. However, it was not only the criminals who were tattooed. Early Japanese history shows non-criminals with tattoos upon their faces and over much of their bodies. Even today, there exists a class of artistic tattoo artists who cover the bodies of their models with elaborate designs. The Japanese gamblers of the feudal period began to have their bodies elaborately tattooed, also. Since the means for tattooing was very rudimentary, the process was time consuming and painful. It was seen as an example of the

Exhibit 3 - Tattoos

individual's strength and courage to have such elaborate tattoos placed on their bodies and to endure the pain over such a long period of time. Although tattooing is today less time consuming and less painful, it is still a mark of respect in the under-world. Some of today's younger members have not submitted to these elaborate tat-toos, however, they still have some sort of smaller singular tattoo on their bodies.

10. The True Ancestors

The true ancestors of the modern Yakuza are the Bakuto and the Tekiya. The Bakuto are the traditional gamblers and the Tekiya, street peddlers. So distinct were the habits of the two groups that Japanese police today still classify most Yakuza members as either Bakuto or Tekiya. The police also utilize a third grouping called Gurental which is composed of later day hoodlums from the period following World War II. The ranks of these three groups are still largely filled by the poor, the landless, the delinquents, and misfits of their society.(18)

Like the Italian Mafia, the Yakuza began organizing in families, with a godfather at the top. The Yakuza added to that structure the unique Japanese relationship known as oyabun-kobun which translates into father-role/child-role. The oyabun provides advice, protection, and help. In return and whenever called for, the oyabun receives unswerving loyalty and service of his kobun.(19)

Inagawa-Kai

Sumiyoshi Rengo

Zen Nihon Rengo-Kai

Kyokuto Sekiguchi Ikka

Early gangster bands were granted a measure of official sanction and became adept at working with authorities. Some oyabun were even deputized. Such agreements with the police often allowed the gangs to consolidate and expand their power.

The early moves by authorities to recognize, work with, and even co-opt the underworld broke important ground. Similiar

Toa Yuai Jigyo Kumiai

agreements later formed the basis for political corruption that today reach the highest levels of Japanese government.(20)

The Yakuza familes have intricate and significant rites which involve the development of brother-like alliances and family secrets. This is not unlike other fraternal and religious organizations such as the Triad Secret Societies of Chinese origin. However, the most glaring dissimilarity is the Yakuza families operate openly and are easily recognizable. Each family even has its own crest. Lapel pins on clothing distinguish family memberships. Logos on buildings and office walls identify ownership and residents. While the Chinese Secret Societies recited poems, used intricate hand signals, and positioned tea cups to make identification known; the Yakuza merely looks to logos or lapel pins for proof of their relationships.

Japanese organized crime cartels have not confined their activities to the islands of Japan. There is ample evidence and documentation they are operating on an international level including the United States.(21)

11. Korean Criminals

For all practical purposes, the Communist government of North Korea has established a closed society which allows no exchange of information with outside countries. While in the south, the Republic of South Korea, a democracy, maintains an equally tight control over both the news media and its publishing houses.(22) The political situation in South Korea is akin to a police state. The press is controlled by the government and thus very little is allowed to be printed that might in some way embarass or discredit the government. However, there is sufficient information available to indicate there exists in Korea organized criminal activity including political corruption - - the mainstay of organized crime everywhere. Organized criminal activities are a reality in South Korea and, as such, are a matter of concern to members of that country's National Assembly.

One Assembly member, Yu Song Hwan, addressed the Assembly on October 13, 1986 and specifically asked questions dealing with criminal gangs, activities, and about the links between the criminals and high government figures.

Kaplan and Dubro, in their book, <u>Yakuza</u>, explore and describe the historical relationship between Japan and Korea. From this historical perspective they expose a Korean band of Yakuza which operates rather openly between the two countries. A very important point is made to the effect that there is no mafia-like commission in existence, the crime groups operate individually and tend to be small and centralized.

Present concerns in most law enforcement agencies appear to be centered on massage parlors, prostitution, and fraudulent marriages. There doesn't seem to be much concern about the future development of the many other criminal enterprises. This lack of concern for the future could be a costly error for law enforcement in the countries where Koreans settle.

The Republic of Korea is a rapidly developing industrialized nation. Corruption of political figures does not seem to be the exception to the rule. There is a historical and present connection with Yakuza of Japan. Korea is a major economic factor in the economy of America. The number of Korean immigrants coming to America has increased from 2,165 in 1965 to an average of 33,445 per year during the 1980's. The Koreans, just as other Asian ethnic groups before them, are relocating in predominately Korean enclaves. As with other Asians, also, they tend to be clannish and stick together. It is this aspect, the ethnic isolation, which makes the Koreans a viable base of exploitation by their own. They are beginning to repeat the resettlement patterns and actions of their predecessors from other East Asian countries.

There is no reason to believe or to expect only law abiding and hard working persons will be immigrating to America. It is reasonable to anticipate the arrival of criminals who will remain within the Korean communities. These criminals will conduct their business and increase their power as they increase their monetary gains. As the number of Koreans coming to this country continues, the operating base for the criminals will increase proportionately. This, in effect, will make the criminals' endeavors much more lucrative.

12. Summary

The Vietnamese criminal groups are in both reorganization and incubation stages. The first masses who were evacuated and the subsequent "escapees" from Vietnam are primarily undocumented people. Their real backgrounds and history are known only to themselves and a select few. It has been relatively easy for many undesireables to enter America and other free countries under the guise of being honest political refugees. It is probably more accurate to classify them as economic refugees. Regardless of their classification, there are a number who have brought with them their criminal expertise which will flourish for them in our open and free society.

Chinese secret societies have as the basis of their origin very noble ideas. Who can find fault with wanting to rid one's nation of foreign rulers? However, we have seen where once this goal has been accomplished and the secret societies which should have dissolved instead developed a power base of their own and thereby had no inclination to give it up. Whether the government assisted or tolerated the existence of the secret societies is irrelevant. The fact remains the secret societies continued to grow and became totally involved in the lucrative fields of vice, narcotics, extortion, labor control, and the usual inevitable corruption. As the geo-political picture changes, these China and Hong Kong based secret societies have spread throughout the world with the Chinese people themselves.

Japanese organized crime groups known to the Japanese police as the "violent ones" and to the rest of the world as Yakuza have a history and tradition constructed by myth and legend. They paint themselves as the Robin Hoods of the East. In reality, they are simply criminals conducting their business for the express purpose of the dual pursuit of profit and power. They have no jurisdictional limitations and they, too, have been expanding throughout the world.

Korean criminal activities in America have been relatively minor in nature when compared to the whole picture of American crime. However, there are certain indications and benchmarks; such as, their Yakuza connection, their vice activity involvement, gambling, and extortion. These should be sufficient to alert law enforcement agencies to aggressively monitor their activities. Such monitoring could retard their evolution to more sophisticated criminal enterprises.

Asian immigration to America has increased dramatically in the past twenty years.(23) It has been common and understandable practice for these newly arrived immigrants to resettle in areas where other immigrants of a similar nationality have previously settled. Such settlement patterns provide a sense of security for the newcomers through cultural and other clan activity.(24) On the other hand, this resettlement pattern is in effect producing ethnic enclaves. This ethnic isolation provides a greater base for criminal exploitation by their own kind. As the base increases so does the activity and the profit. With profit comes power - greater the profit the greater the power.

Today, the various ethnic Asian communities in America and elsewhere are providing fertile grounds for ethnic criminals to cultivate and harvest the fruits of their labors. The classic pattern of organized crime will continue to be perpetuated by these new inhabitants until law enforcement is successful in addressing this new crime problem.

Notes   (1) See Alfred McCoy, <u>The Politics of Heroin in Southeast Asia</u>. McCoy's book meticulously details these officials and their criminal involvement with opium and heroin.

(2) <u>Author</u>: What we don't see or hear is what has been told to me by hundreds of Vietnamese and other Southeast Asian refugees during the past four years. Their stories are the same and are almost unbelievable. These people only ask that I not identify them. They do not want to go on television or radio. They will not talk to the media. They are afraid. They fear retaliation to themselves or in some cases to their family members who remain in Vietnam. I respect their wishes for anonymity. I respect the confidences of those past and present employees of our government agencies who assure me the Vietnamese claims are very plausible and probably very accurate.

(3) W.P. Morgan, <u>Triad Societies of Hong Kong</u>, The Government Printer, Hong Kong, 1982, P. xiv.

(4) From a 1983 presentation given in Washington, D.C. on Triad Societies by Inspector Sydney Chou, Triad Bureau, Hong Kong Police.

(5) See W.P. Morgan, <u>Triad Societies,</u> p. xiv.

Notes (6) Harold Irwin Cleveland, <u>Massacres of Christians by Heathen Chinese and Horrors of The Boxers</u>, Butler and Alger, New Haven, Conn., 1900.

(7) See W.P. Morgan, <u>Triad Societies</u>, p. 3.

(8) Ibid. pp. 60-63.

(9) This was stated in an official brief prepared for the President's Commission on Organized Crime by the Criminal Intelligence Bureau, Police Headquarters, Hong Kong, October, 1984, pp. 15-17.

(10) Ibid. p. 17.

(11) Chuk Luen Bong, Royal Hong Kong Police Department, September, 1984.

(12) Fenton Bresler, <u>The Chinese Mafia</u>. The quotation was taken from Bresler's presentation before the President's Commission on Organized Crime, Record of Hearings III, October 23-25, 1984, pp. 427-433.

(13) President's Commission on Organized Crime, record of Hearings III, October 23-25, 1984, pp. 447-451, 453-459, 461-464, and 473-475.

(14) David E. Kaplan and Alex Dubro, <u>Yakuza: The Explosive Account of Japan's Criminal Underworld</u>, Addison-Wesley Publishing Company, Inc., Reading, Mass., 1986, p. 24.

(15) Ibid. p. 24.

(16) Ibid.

Notes   (17) These characteristics are also graphically displayed in the 1975 movie, <u>Yakuza</u>, starring actor Robert Mitchum.

(18) Ibid. p. 18.

(19) Ibid. p. 18-19.

(20) Ibid. p 26-27.

(21) A case of major proportions substantiating this statement is discussed in Chapter Five of this book.

(22) <u>Author</u>: When I first began research for this book, I found there was very little written concerning Korean criminal activities. This lack of information seems to be due primarily to the political situations in both North and South Korea.

(23) See Appendix A-2 for a display of select Asian immigrants admitted to the United States from 1965 through 1984 by country of birth.

(24) See Appendix A-3 for a display of immigrant settlement patterns in the United States by the year 1984.

CHAPTER TWO

The subject of gangs always seems to surface in public discussions or in news articles dealing with Asian crime. This is only right as these gangs are obviously an important segment of Asian society. Many oriental communities, such as Korean, Chinese, or Vietnamese, have their street gangs. These gangs are readily recognized by the people with whom they share the same geographical and ethnic origins when they come in contact with them on the street and in their businesses.

1. Adult Gangs

No one, either in law enforcement or in the Asian communities, disputes the existence of these Asian gangs. They are known for what they are: hardened criminals who will stop at nothing to assert their strength and criminality and to take from the community what wealth is available. The people in the community, who must face them as part of doing business, see them as men of prey and skilled at the practice of extortion, arson, and even murder. They are not teen-age gangs or 'youth' as some in the news media have made them out to be. When their ages are documented they are most often found to be full grown men and a few of their number have military experience.

Law enforcement practitioners experienced in the field of Asian crime generally agree the term 'youth', when used in describing these Asian gangs, is a misnomer in the classic sense of the meaning.(1) This term gives the wrong message and image to the public and should cease being a way of describing gang members.

Certainly, law enforcement investigators and intelligence officers should never describe them as youth when writing street reports, providing assessments, or making comments to the press.

Nearly all members of these various oriental gangs fail to meet the common definition of the term, youth. The period of youth is thought to be the time of life between childhood and adulthood; a time of development physically, emotionally, psychologically, and morally. Generally, the age of youth ends when the age of majority has been reached which by law, in some states and nations, is at some point after the eighteenth birthday.(2)

A gang is a group of people who are joined together for illegal and disruptive purposes. It is the purpose of the organization which justifies its classification as a gang. In community business areas it is not uncommon to find groups of Asian young people hanging around together. Casual as they may be and appear, most often one person dominates and assumes the quasi leadership of the group. From this loose knit relationship comes parties, sports, and other social activities. Social groups become criminal gangs when they turn from purely social activities to criminal pursuits in the community.

Often the criminal gangs can be found to have recognized leaders who enforce discipline and control the membership. More often than not the gangs are recognized as controlling a certain geographical area known to the underworld as turf.

2. Vietnamese Gangs

Vietnamese gangs can be and most often are classified by their organization and structure. Investigators who have been involved with these gangs, since their arrival in the United States, report they can be classified into three distinct groups; formal, informal, and casual. Few Vietnamese communities, however, will have all three. Nearly always, Vietnamese business and residential areas will have at least one form of these gangs in full operation.(3)

0   Formal Gangs

Formal gangs are those which have a definitive leader, a solid core of reliable and available members, and a geographical area and/or criminal activity under their control.

0   Informal Gangs

Informal gangs are by comparison to formal ones, new, loosely organized, and less focused. They often have a charasmatic individual in his late 20's to mid-30's who strives to establish himself as the leader.   He acts as an 'older brother' advising his followers as to how they should perform.   Some leaders will provide only guidance to the group and will never actually participate in the criminal activity beyond the planning phase.(4)   It has been found, in some cases, that the 'elder brother' is actually receiving instructions and guidance from yet another individual in his senior years. The gang's elder statesman is thought of as the 'uncle.' However, the terms, 'elder brother' and 'uncle' do not necessarily reflect any blood or legal relationship. It is simply the practice of Vietnamese to identify and clarify certain personal relationships by describing them in familial terms.

The ages of members in informal gangs varies from teens to twenties. The fluctuation in membership size and the spread of membership ages are probably the two most important blockages toward their building a more dynamic and ongoing organization. This lack of organization further denies them the ability to control a turf and/or specific criminal activity.

0   Casual Gangs

Casual gangs are thought of as groups of persons, mostly males, who habitually band together. They are, for the most part, leaderless and make their decisions to commit crimes by mutual discussion and agreement. They are free-lancers who target their victims because of the victim's perceived wealth and availability. Sometimes, they will leave their home turf for distant locations to attack victims at the request of the leaders of formal gangs.

It should not be assumed the lack of organization or strong leadership renders the casual gangs any less effective than the more obvious formal Asian gangs. There exists extensive evidence that the disorganized and loosely knit 'casual gang' robs and kills as effectively as their formal gang counterparts. In fact, their randomness can even be more feared in the community and more difficult to investigate by law enforcement officials.

3. Survivors of War

In any description of Vietnamese gangs there are certain phenomena which must be addressed. The individual gang members and the existence of the gangs themselves can be best understood when looking at them from a historical, political, and cultural perspective. It is emphasized here that this understanding in no way, manner, shape, or form excuses or gives tacit approval for their anti-social and disruptive criminal behavior. It merely attempts to explain why these refugees embark on such a life cycle after they arrive in the United States and in other free world nations.

People who have never experienced war on their own land are extremely fortunate. The native born Vietnamese comes from an environment where war was a continual way of life. In trying to understand the Vietnamese criminals' ruthless behavior, it must be remembered nearly all of them have survived hell in their own lifetimes.(5)

A Vietnamese man about 35 years of age once said, "From the time I was conceived, I heard guns being fired and bombs exploding." Death and destruction were commonplace with survival being the ultimate goal in his life. His aim never included a retirement plan, pension, or social security. His concern was immediate survival for he and his family - - one day at a time. On another occasion, an elderly Chinese lady said about the Vietnamese, in general, "Because of all the wars over their years and lifetimes, the Vietnamese have lost part of their natural nature, kindness, and gentleness."(6)

The two statements above, poetic and self-serving as they may have been, shed some light, understanding, and, hopefully, an appreciation for the violence which lies just below the surface for many Vietnamese. It is something every law enforcement officer must be aware of and must understand. It is no secret among officers who investigate crimes every day in the Vietnamese community that the Vietnamese criminal sees law enforcement as the enemy and does not see them as preservers of the peace. He, the criminal, wants instant gratification. He wants to survive the day - - the moment. His small stature and broad smile must not be misread for the friendly picture it depicts can be easily misleading. Rather, the Vietnamese criminal should be thought of as a recently programmed individual whose skills relate more to countering corrupt police and fighting the enemy with garrot and bomb than making his peaceful and productive way in his new homeland.

4. The Mobility Factor

There is another aspect of uniqueness with the Vietnamese, particularly the unattached and disenfranchised ones. It is their mobility. As with nearly all Americans, they enjoy the ability to drive with great ease and frequency to any point they desire. There is ample evidence that one core group of Vietnamese criminals recently travelled about America committing crimes as they went and all the while avoided arrest through a series of maneuvers that baffled police everywhere.

Beginning in 1985, they struck in Texas, Louisiana, Virginia, South Dakota, and Canada. Their mobile crime spree ended in Virginia in 1986. During their travels they committed crimes wherever Vietnamese lived in groups. They were responsible for auto theft, robbery, larceny, shootings, forgery, and the cashing of stolen checks.(7)

Most gang members have no immediate family, jobs, or other ties. Having few or no roots, they are able to move about without family or community controls of any kind. Almost always their crime activities will take them from one 'little Saigon' to another which means using a gang member's car or stealing one for the trip. Regardless of where they go, they will find their new location a familiar and safe haven against the greater community and its law enforcement officers.

5. Teaming with Friends

The newly arrived male who lacks a family, business, education, or wealth, will nearly always turn to friends to see him through his first days in his new home. Generally, he will seek out someone he met while in a refugee camp or find another male he knew from his native village. Like most human beings, he needs immediate company and comfort since now he faces a new form of challenge on just getting settled. When he first reaches the street, he immediately sees that few understand his language, his culture, or his needs. One or two friends can provide him with the solace to get him through the first and worst days of being alone in this strange land.

This ease of mobility, plus the knowledge of an existing 'friend' or 'brother' in other cities, makes fleeing a so-called 'hot' area for a 'cool' one a relatively easy and safe option.

These rootless and disenfranchised Vietnamese who are often alone and who lack job skills and education are easy prey for some 'elder brother' trying to establish himself as a gang leader. Existing Asian gangs like to open their arms to these newly arrived nomads and provide them with family and brotherhood. Both parties gain. The existing gang gets a loyal new member who adds to their number and strength. At the same time, the new member acquires a 'family' and acceptance. The Vietnamese criminals have also been accepted outside their own ethnic criminal groups, as well. New York City investigators report that Chinese crime groups known to them as the Ghost Shadows and the Flying Dragons have been recruiting Vietnamese criminals and their associates to aid the Chinese with their own crime needs. In San Francisco, according to one former investigator, Vietnamese of Chinese descent have been admitted to the ranks of the Wah Ching, a major Chinese street gang.(8)

What is most interesting is the similarity of the Vietnamese gangs, their activities, membership, structure, and organization. Whether the gangs are in California, Oregon, Texas, Louisiana, Illinois, Massachusetts, New York, Virginia, or Canada, they are basically the same. Some are more sophisticated and some are better organized but they all pose threats in varying degrees to the peace and security of the community. There is no question as to the existence of the gangs. The question pertains to the extent of their development and the influence they exert on their surrounding community.

Equally as interesting as Vietnamese gangs in North America is the report compiled by the Australian Victoria Police Force. They concluded, "...It can be seen from the history of the Vietnamese gangs in Victoria and their associated involvement in criminal activities coupled with a reluctance of victims to cooperate with authorities, that the task of policing these gangs is an extremely daunting one. The problems we are currently facing are language and culture, similar to those in America ..." The conclusion of the Victoria paper relates to reports being made in the United States and Canada, such as: "...the gangs are still in their infancy, they have strong connections with other gangs in other parts of Australia, the mobility of the gang members is a phenomenon there just like here . . ." The author's final statement was one of great concern which mirrors many of the apprehensions felt by law enforcement officers in the United States. The paper estimated that ". . . approximately 86,000 Vietnamese are now resident in Australia, and, of these, 28,000 reside in Victoria, with an estimated additional 80,000 awaiting resettlement in Australia in the near future. This increasing population will provide a greater scope of activities for the gangs' operation thus compounding this problem already in existence."(9)(10)

6. Regarding Cowboys, Frogmen, and Fishermen

More often than not, a Vietnamese gang will be known in the Vietnamese community only by its leader's name. If the given name of the leader is "Tho," the gang will be known as "Tho's gang" or "Tho's group." If, for one reason or another, the leader, Tho, is removed from the group, the gang will continue to be known as "Tho's group" providing, that is, the remaining central gang members remain in place. Should all of the leadership change and a new group be formed, a new name may or may not be adopted.

Some Vietnamese gangs will give themselves a name with a special meaning reflecting certain prowess or descriptive of their home area. Others may name themselves after a particularly strong or cunning animal or take a name from Vietnamese myth and legend.(11) Unique also is their use of terms to identify the training, occupation, and other characteristics of the different members or their most prominent leaders. They may also pick a name which would conjure up fear in the hearts and minds of those in the community they plan to extort.

Very few law enforcement officers and fewer yet of the media have learned not to be too narrow in their interpretation of the meaning of titles used by the Vietnamese. Few among the Vietnamese gang watchers and investigators seem to be aware that the gangs' chosen names represent little more than monikers around which to rally.

The American press and law enforcement, in their efforts to be concise and specific, have done themselves a disservice and added to the already convoluted picture of Vietnamese gangs by classifying the several groups as belonging to the Frogmen, Fishermen, and the Cowboys. When the news media uses these terms, (as do many law enforcement officers in their reports, as well,) they are most often additionally emphasized by stating these group names in upper case letters.

According to testimony given before the President's Commission on Organized crime, the so-called Frogmen appear to be nothing more than a generic term attached to military-trained, underwater demolition members formerly associated with U.S. combat troops during the Vietnam War. It is generic in that some Frogmen associates were, in fact, members of the Vietnamese Air Force and Army.

According to another witness at the same hearing, the Fisherman gang of Texas was a title given to a group of criminals who were, in fact, acting in concert. Several of the group had been, indeed, fishermen by vocation. The gang had never assumed the name, Fishermen, nor did they ever write or speak using such a title. It was picked up from the generic use of the word by the Vietnamese when responding to police interrogation regarding their present and former occupations.(12)

Cowboys is perhaps the name most commonly associated with Vietnamese gangs. This, too, is a generic term. It describes the restless attitude of those who cause trouble and who, among the males in the Vietnamese community, do not conform to the rules of society.(13) It is normal to use the term, in a general sense, similar to the use of the word when describing a new police officer as a "hot shot" or "hot dog."

Although this may seem to be relatively insignificant and by some to be making a mountain out of the proverbial mole hill, it is neither. At a time when law enforcement is trying to build their credibility with the Vietnamese community the use of such terms, in the wrong context, has a very negative effect on the people involved. It can also give law enforcement a picture that is not a true representation of what is going on inside the Vietnamese community.

Law enforcement and the news media must control their seemingly natural inclination to label and place everything in neat little categories or self-explaining boxes.

7. Chinese Criminal Gangs

Chinese crime organizations are formal gangs in the classic sense of the meaning. In nearly every case in which a Chinese gang has been analyzed, it has had the following five characteristics:(14)

- 0 Recognized leadership
- 0 Well marked turf
- 0 Strict code of discipline
- 0 Emphasis on silence
- 0 Organization

A typical Chinese gang organization is shown in Exhibit 1. The original of this chart was presented to the United States Senate Permanent Subcommittee on Investigations Hearings on Emerging Asian Criminal Groups, in September 1986, by former Inspector John McKenna, Supervisor, Asian Gang Task Force, San Francisco Police Department.

McKenna's testimony went into detail about the structure, organization, and activities of the Wah Ching, the predominant power in San Francisco's Chinatown.

He stated, "They start out as loosely organized street kids and graduate into a cell-like unit. This unit is controlled by others who have graduated from the cells. They started by extorting money from local shopkeepers and eventually began to take a percentage of business profits. No gambling house operated without paying a percentage. Often winners would be robbed on their way home after a successful night in the gambling house. They (Wah Ching Gang) then graduate from this type of gambling houses, to prostitution houses, and similar type businesses. Profits from these illegitimate enterprises are often invested in and operate all kinds of legitimate businesses."

Unfortunately, this type of activity and gang structure is not restricted to San Francisco. The Chinese Street Gangs, Ghost Shadows and Flying Dragons, are known to exist and operate in nearly every major Chinese community in the United States and Canada. They, too, are involved in the entertainment industries, gambling, prostitution, and narcotics trafficking. It is well known that these gangs can be vicious and are prone to erupt into violence at any time. When these eruptions do take place, their targets, or worse yet, those persons in close proximity to their targets, fall victim also.

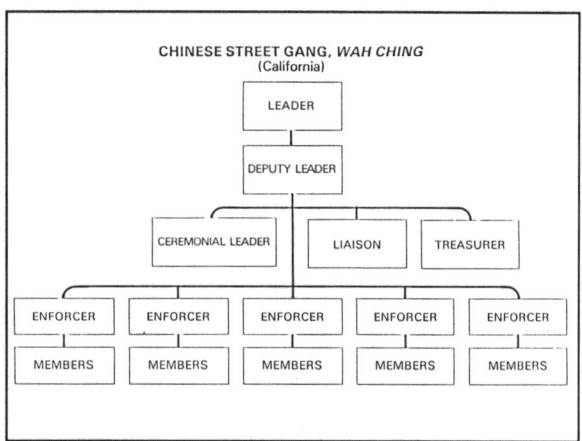

Exhibit 1 - *Wah Ching* Organization

8.   Chinese as Traditional Organized Crime

Chinese gangs have a long and standing reputation for tight organization and affiliation with international Chinese associations that span the world. Their manner of conducting business and their affiliations were presented in testimony before the

President's Commission on Organized Crime in New York. The gangs, Ghost Shadows, the Flying Dragons, and their respective affiliate Tongs, the On Leong and the Hip Sing, were the subject of long discussions by law enforcement experts testifying at the Hearings.

The Washington Times newspaper ran a series of articles in 1986 in which these gangs were again identified as having chapters in such major cities as Washington, D.C., Baltimore, Atlanta, Boston, Chicago, New York, Minneapolis, and San Francisco. In each of these cities were located both the On Leong Tong and Hip Sing Tong organizations. The article also stated the gangs were involved in drugs, murders, robbery, extortion, kidnapping, prostitution, and loan sharking. Many of the gang members, the article reported, served as couriers and were used by the

Exhibit 2 - New York City   Exhibit 3 - 5th Precinct

Tongs as street sellers of heroin and other drugs.(15)

 The descriptive nomenclature, Street Gang, may portray the picture of these Chinese Gangs as just a bunch of thugs roaming and terrorizing only the Chinese living in the Chinese enclaves of America's inner cities. This is not the case since these so-called 'Street Gangs' are, in reality, organized criminal enterprises in existence for the purpose of maintaining, perpetuating, and furthering their control over a community's vice and drug activity. When allowed to follow their desired course of action, they quickly acquire great wealth, avoid taxes, invest in legitimate business, undersell, and ultimately drive out of business those who cannot compete with the available money of the Chinese. They also position themselves financially for corrupting persons in government and elsewhere. In due time, certain members of the Chinese gangs are accepted into the legitimate community

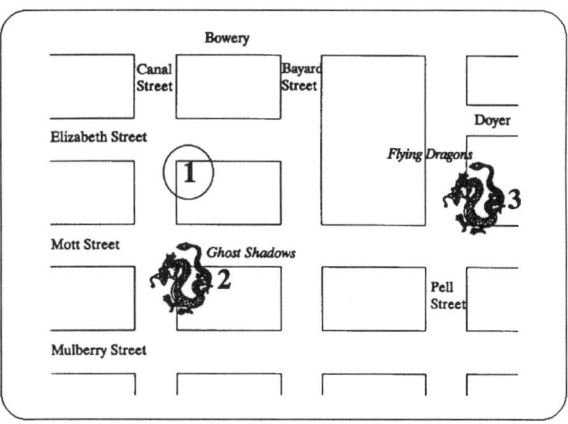

Exhibit 4 - New York City Chinatown

as leading citizens having acquired their new positions by way of organized crime and immunity to the law. As 'respectable' citizens they are better able to guide their business operations so that others among them may be helped and positioned, also. In this way, each new recruit adds to and furthers the strength of the overall criminal effort. The streets of New York City's Chinatown are examples of one such gang growth and organization. Here, at the very doorstep of the Police Department's 5th Precinct shown on the map at circle #1, operate two of the nation's most notorious Chinese gangs, the Flying Dragons and the Ghost Shadows. Two blocks apart are the headquarters of two Tongs, On Leong Tong at #2, and Hip Sing Tong shown in position #3 in Exhibit 4.

9. Korean Gangs

The most difficult oriental ethnic group to study among the Asian gangs is that of the Koreans. And it is probably the least documented by both law enforcement and the news media. In 1985, the Federal Bureau of Investigation published results of a research project which they titled, <u>Oriental Organized Crime</u>. Little was said about Korean crime activity in the United States except to report the Koreans were committing crimes and avoiding arrests, for the most part. Other writers have taken a more serious stance, however, and have made awareness of Korean gang crime a subject for local law enforcement training.

In 1983, the Los Angeles Police Department developed and delivered training constructed around the following facts:

0	Identification	- Korean gang members are not easy to identify, yet they have formed criminal networks within U.S. cities.
0	Linkage	- Korean gang members have been linked to Japanese (*Yakuza*) and Armenian organized crime.
0	Well Armed	- Gang members are often well armed. They obtain their weapons from residential burglaries. In Los Angeles they seem to prefer 45 automatics and 30.06 rifles.
0	Interstate	- Interstate contact between gangs is increasing. For example, they have been seen with the Eagle crime group in Hawaii and New York's Korean Power and White Tigers groups.

In 1986, the U.S. Immigration and Naturalization Service wrote: "Korean rings have been found responsible for prostitution networks and narcotics smuggling schemes. A major investigation in New York City, completed in 1984, pointed to an elaborate scheme of bribery, smuggling, credit card fraud, and police corruption in furtherance of their operation of a number of massage parlors used as fronts for prostitution."(16) This example is described further in Chapter Five of this handbook.

In a 1987 article in Woman's World magazine, Author P.F Burns wrote extensively about Korean women being sold into slavery. He described how Korean organized crime in Houston, Texas, worked behind the fronts of modeling studios and massage parlors, all the while trafficking in sex slavery. ". . . and more shocking still, almost all of them came here (United States) as wives of returning American servicemen."(17)

In the same P.F. Burns article, the U.S. Immigration and Naturalization Service was quoted as saying an estimated 90 percent of all Korean prostitutes in the United States came here as wives of service personnel. The Service reported that nearly 3,000 of the 20,000 military personnel returning from that country during the period studied brought Korean wives with them.

Houston, Texas, Vice Officer Oscar Farrell, an expert on Korean prostitution rings, stated in the same Burns article, "They are shipped right to the modeling studio or massage parlor to perform sexual favors for cash." Farrell added, "Korean recruiters come by (the girls residences) while their husbands are away, maybe even overseas, and say, "Hey, you can make big money in New York and if you don't have the money, I'll lend it to you." They go thinking they're going to rub backs, but then they're forced to do other things."

According to the U.S. Immigration and Naturalization Service the girls are sometimes swapped from house to house in a city and sometimes even from one city to another. One Washington State Sheriff's Department officer commented that a Korean prostitute working in Tacoma (Washington State) may turn up later working in a house of prostitution in Alaska.(18)

According to literature published by the Los Angeles Police Department, "Korean gangs are structured and operate through a blend of old world values and the realities of life in a liberal new society. They are, for the the most part, totally different from conventional street gangs. Since the inception of the Korean Killers during the mid 1970's, several other Korean gangs have been formed. All operate along similar lines and friendly interaction is common . . . Korean gang members are involved in varied criminal activity including narcotics, armed robbery, extortion, rape, burglary, etc. The older gang members have attempted to establish interstate narcotics connections. Korean gangs are both sophisticated and innovative and they will venture into new fields that appear to offer acceptable margins of profit."(19)

Although Korean gangs have not yet gained much reputation for being as dangerous as their Vietnamese and Chinese counterparts, there is growing evidence to substantiate their existence and criminal activity. The fact that they have not yet gotten the public attention is to their distinct advantage in that it allows them to continue to operate and grow in strength all the while unpursued and underestimated.(20)

10. Asian Gang Recruitment

Perhaps the most distressing fact regarding Asian gangs is that gang leadership and gang recruiters have a seemingly bottomless pool of potential recruits to draw upon for their membership. As law enforcement officers there is little that can presently be done to effectively impact the size of the standby recruits. If it is true that little can now be implemented to turn new gang recruits around, then law enforcement must rely upon this awareness of the recruit problem and attempt to use it to some advantage to the justice system. Several suggestions include:(21)

0   Dedicate criminal intelligence effort to identify recruiters

Most major city police departments have criminal intelligence units which could be partially committed to the growing crime problems related to Asian gangs. With proper targeting on Asian gang leadership and recruitment, some of the problems related to continued gang membership growth might be controlled - - even reduced. The cost of adding Asian gang leadership and recruiters to a department's mission would be small when compared to the annual cost to a community in lost revenue, jobs, and general security the gangs cause through their criminal activities.

0   Assign foot patrol officer to Asian community

The daily presence of uniformed and plain clothes officers in Asian business and residential areas can have marked affect on whether Asian criminals will target a community. Those communities with foot patrols during business hours most always show a decline in extortions and other crimes.

0   Expand law enforcement training in Asian culture, language, etc.

Very few police academies and inservice programs are presently teaching techniques for dealing with the emerging Asian crime problems. Training should be required in the proper approach for addressing Asian elders, the denial of gifts, the correct use of names, and how to handle problems that may seem ordinary to law enforcement personnnel but cause unnecessary loss of face for involved Asians.

0   Involve Asian community leaders in crime prevention

It is a fact that many Asians are not accustomed to honest law enforcement officers and honest government at any level. Asian elders and business leaders should be encouraged to participate in 'ride-along' programs, to sit on committees during which police services are being discussed and assigned. Lastly, they should be encouraged to assist investigators by encouraging members of their communities to provide both public and confidential information in order to prevent future crimes.

0   Draw law enforcement recruits from Asian population

Focussed recruitment should be undertaken in order to involve more Asian citizens in all aspects of law enforcement. At the present time, many Asian citizens have a low opinion of law enforcement which is fueled by their past experiences in Vietnam, China, Korea, Laos and elsewhere in Asia. They should be encouraged to participate as officers and members of the civilian staffs of law enforcement agencies for the good of their own people and for the community at large.

0   Enlist media assistance in public awareness effort

The media can have a great affect on how an Asian community sees its role in the government process and what the people imagine the police services are doing on their behalf. To improve the status of law enforcement services in the eyes of the Asian communty, the media should be encouraged to cover the various aspects of crime prevention and the importance all individuals play in reducing community crime.

11. The Recruiter

A gang recruiter can be any person in a particular Asian gang. For all purposes, all gang members are potential recruiters. Most often it is the gang member who spots or chances upon a likely candidate for membership and, thus, becomes the recruiter of the moment. Once spotted as meeting the gang's minimum standards, the gang member goes after the recruit. The recruiter feathers his own nest if he is able to successfully recruit a new member who turns out to be both loyal and dependable. Of course, when the recruiter manages to spot and recruit several new members who prove beneficial to the overall criminal effort of the Asian gang he has improved his position with each new addition to the group. The recruiters are not altruistic individuals who are looking for some worthy individual to whom they can give a better and more meaningful life. The gang recruiter is primarily interested in caring for his own needs and in building his own position inside the gang. He never forgets that his own quality of life is highly dependent on the size and influence of the gang to which he belongs. He also knows that new members make the gang larger in number and great numbers always result in greater gang strength. Good recruiters are to Asian gangs what good personnel officers are to businesses.

The successful recruit, on the other hand, attempts to ingratiate his recruiter and, by doing this, becomes accepted by other gang members and finally the gang's leader. The new recruit shows his enthusiasm for serving the gang by doing whatever the gang's leader dictates.

Good targets for recruitment appear to be from two distinct groups and possess one common denominator. The common denominator - - family. The first group is made up of young men who, for one reason or another, have become emotionally and psychologically distanced from their family. The second group is made up of youths who have no immediate family, such as the unaccompanied young adults fleeing Vietnam. To these potential gang members, gang recruiters often represent "elder brothers" and their gangs "the families." Blood oaths and secret swearing-in ceremonies further reinforce the families' togetherness, strength, and loyalty. The bond soon becomes almost unbreakable between the new member, his recruiter, and the gang.

This may be a simplistic explanation of understanding the recruitment and gang member relationships and is offered here only to put the relationship aspect into perspective. Other factors, such as peer group pressure, self-worth, need for family, and acceptance into a social structure also play an important part in these recruitment dynamics.

The existing Chinese street gangs are currently taking in young Vietnamese to be their soldiers and enforcers. This is a very beneficial arrangement for both the Chinese gang and the sought-after Vietnamese. First, the Chinese gang benefits from the general reputation of having on-call a number of violence prone Vietnamese. This adds to the Chinese gang's overall reputation of strength especially when a neighboring Chinese gang may not have any Vietnamese members among its soldiers. For the recruited Vietnamese, the Chinese gang serves as the immediate nuclear family which the young adult Vietnamese left behind in Vietnam. It also gives the recruit acceptance, inflates his ego, and makes him feel like a useful person. It gives him meaning because he now has status in the eyes of his friends who now see him as employed and enjoying all the benefits that go with membership in a Chinese gang.

12. Summary

Asian gangs, representative of different ethnic groups, do exist. They are at various stages of development and organization and stay primarily within the confines of their own particular ethnic groups. However, as gang members grow older, they do not necessarily mature out of the gang but rather relinquish their line duties as enforcers and runners for new positions as operators. Eventually, the best of them elevate into so-called legitimate businessmen.

Asian street gangs are nothing more than the minor leagues of professional organized crime. Just as the privates and sergeants are the necessary work force of armies so, too, are the ordinary street gang members the laborers for organized crime.

It has often been suggested that law enforcement should design a profile to help identify the highly mobile Asian criminals travelling across the country and even from nation to nation. This is possible and could be done but only after significant data has been accumulated and analysed. A tool such as this could be very useful especially for uniformed police who patrol not only the Asian communities of the world but also the main highway carrying the criminals from one Asian community to another.

Exhibit 5 - Chinese Arch, Washington, D.C.

Notes   (1) <u>Author</u>: In discussions, with detectives and police officers across the United States and in Canada, one is constantly reminded that Asian gang members are seldom teenagers and the vast majority are adults beyond their formative years.

(2) This American form of classifying age and defining adulthood does not carry over into the Asian community. To a great extent, many Asians are accustomed to treating males as 'boys' or 'youth' who do not hold positions of importance, lack marital status, or have little education. When investigators discuss certain Asian criminals with members of the Asian community, the citizens are apt to reflect on the subjects of their conversation as 'bad boys.'

(3) The basis for this statement comes from reports collected from the main Vietnamese communities in the United States and Canada.

(4) <u>Author</u>: This was the case in Arlington, Virginia, where a gang's leader had legitimate work while providing the gang with both direction and organization. It was the leader's belief that he was beyond the reach of the law as long as he maintained his community job and never participated in the gang's crimes or received any stipend from their crime activity.

(5) For a comprehensive reading of the turmoils and conflicts experienced by Vietnamese citizens during that country's several wars, read: <u>Vietnam:</u>

Notes   <u>A Political History</u>, by Joseph Buttinger, Praeger Publishers, New York, 1972.

(6) <u>Author</u>: These are direct quotes taken from persons I have interviewed. All have asked they remain anonymous.

(7) <u>Author</u>: I appeared before the U.S. Senate Permanent Subcommittee on Investigations, Hearings on Emerging Ethnic Criminal Groups in September, 1986 and gave this report.

(8)   According to retired San Francisco Police Inspector John McKenna, San Francisco Police Department, San Francisco, California, in his testimony before the U.S. Senate Permanent Subcommittee on Investigation, September, 1986.

(9)   Excerpts from the Victoria Police Force in Australia. Report entitled: <u>A Profile of Vietnamese Gang Activity in Victoria, 1982-86</u>.

(10)   U.S. Newsweek magazine, <u>The Gangs of Asia</u>, April 2, 1985, p.2.

(11)   See President's Commission on Organized Crime, Record of Hearing III, Organized Crime of Asian origin, p.498, from a statement by Donald Saviers, October 17, 1984.

(12)   At the conclusion of the President's Commission on Organized Crime, Asian Hearings, a newspaper reporter asked former Houston Police Officer Robert Casey to discuss a Vietnamese crime gang in Houston, Texas. He emphatically denied the existence of such a group. He advised the media the group's name stood for nothing more than the occupation of several of the group's members.

Notes   (13) <u>Author</u>: I first heard the term, Cowboy, while serving with the U.S. Marine Corps in Danang. It was a term given to those who served mainly in Saigon proper and were thus far from the fighting in the bush. The Vietnamese Army used the term also for their troops stationed away from the front.   It was years later when I learned the word is actually the American phonetic pronounciation of the Vietnamese words, *cao boi*, which the Vietnamese use to describe 'bad boys', i.e., trouble makers and delinquents as they are known in western culture.

(14)   U.S. Senate, John McKenna. Ibid.

(15)   Jerry Seper, <u>Asian Crime in America</u>, Washington Times, January, 1986.

(16)   U.S. Immigration and Naturalization Service, case summary, October 8, 1986.

(17)   P.F. Burns, <u>Sold Into Slavery</u>, Woman's World, 10-24-87, p.41.

(18)   Ibid.

(19)   Bulletin, Los Angeles Police Department, 1986.

(20)   The San Bernardino County Sheriff's Department, California, issued an unclassified training bulletin regarding oriental gangs for their deputies in January, 1987.   Their Intelligence Division stated that local Korean youth banded together to protect themselves from "menacing Hispanic gangs." These Koreans, the report went on, later became a criminal gang when its members turned to burglarizing homes of local Korean families

Notes   followed by their dealing in narcotics and weapons and sexually assaulting Korean women.   The report stated the Korean youth gangs do not wear distinctive clothing or tattoos and that gang warfare between them and other gangs is virtually unknown.

(21) Suggestions by Jack Morris, Manager, Criminal Intelligence, Bureau of Organized Crime and Criminal Intelligence, California Department of Justice, January 5, 1988.

CHAPTER THREE

This chapter describes actual situations in which Asian gangs have committed major crimes. It is offered here to give readers insight into how Asian criminals plan and execute their crimes and make good their escapes. Most often, as readers will see, the criminals are successful in all three phases of their operations. As the result of reading this handbook, it is hoped the reasons for their frequent successes will become readily apparent and counter strategies will be conceived and developed by law enforcement.

It should be understood, also, that the following criminal activities in no way cover all of the unlawful acts involving Asian gangs in the countries in which they have settled.

1. Extortion - The Six Tables Approach

The gang's target was a small, family run, Vietnamese restaurant located near the center of the town's 'Little Saigon'. The results might have been the same had this group set their sights on a Chinese or Korean restaurant. The important fact is that the restaurant was Asian and that was all that mattered. The six member gang of Vietnamese criminals collected in front of the restaurant at four in the afternoon. When they were assembled, they followed their leader through the restaurant's main entrance.

Even though the six had entered, one after the other, and were obviously together, they broke apart once inside with each moving toward one of the restaurant's six tables. No patrons were inside when they entered so they now, for all purposes, had the merchant's entire restaurant fully occupied. Each sat quietly studying the menu and making independent decisions as to what food to order. When they were waited on, they ordered food and drink as any customer would be expected to do. They carried on normal conversations, as they ate, across the tables without causing a disturbance of any kind. To the uninitiated person in Asian extortion practices, the six young men appeared normal in every respect. Had a non-Asian or untrained police officer happened in, the visitor would have found little or no evidence that a major crime was taking place.

The process of ordering, eating, and talking led also to ordering and consuming beer and still the six did not come together at one table. Dinner for the six Vietnamese gang members took nearly two hours. While they sat and took their time over their meals and beers, other customers entered, saw the six, and left quickly most likely for an eatery with a less threatening clientele.

It was noted later that the six had been dressed in blue jeans, slacks, and an otherwise mixture of 'mod' clothes that did not relate to their being students or business persons. What bothered the restaurant manager the most was the fact the six had entered at exactly the moment when the restaurant normally enjoyed its peak business of the day; four to six o'clock in the afternoon.

Once their dinners were finished, they began requesting their bills. The waitress was happy to comply and moved forward and handed one of the men his ticket. He refused it and asked her to give his check to a man at one of the other tables. She complied and the man at the table accepted the check without argument. In short order, she was requested by the other four men to give the same man their checks, as well.

Now holding all six checks, the man turned to the waitress and, in a very pleasant manner, requested to have the restaurant's owner brought to his table.

The waitress stepped through the office door and soon a Vietnamese man in his fifties came over to the table where the man sat holding the six checks. As the owner approached, the man with the checks got quickly to his feet, bowed in respect to the Vietnamese elder, and greeted him as 'Uncle.' The owner bowed slightly in return and greeted the gang member as 'nephew.'

"We are out of jobs," the gang member said, "and we have no money and no families. We are alone in America. We like your restaurant and would like to eat here regularly."

The restaurant owner listened as he glanced about at the other men who sat silently at the five other tables. He knew now what he was up against as he glanced about at the five men listening to the conversation between their leader and himself. It was the familiar extortion game he had seen or heard about in Vietnam. Thoughts of vandalism, fire, harrassments, and even attacks on he and his family raced through his mind. He fought to retain his smile less he give away his real fear. Then he looked back into the cool eyes of the man holding the six tickets.

The gang member then suggested the owner overlook their present six checks for food and drinks out of kindness toward them. He waved his arm around the room to point out there had been no other business while the six ate. He was attempting to get the point across that their visits might reoccur again, at peak business time, should the owner's answer be less than satisfactory.

"It was because we sat separately that you had no business, Uncle. We will be happy to sit together the next time we visit your business if you like." The man doing the talking smiled and was very polite. The owner agreed and thanked them for paying him a visit. He picked up the six checks while telling them there would be no charge whenever they again chose his restaurant for their meals.

0   Observation

For nearly half a year the six gang members visited the restaurant each time they were in the area. They always sat together while they ate the best food on the menu and drank their choice of drinks. Never once did they pay for a single meal. The owner was pleased because he had no vandalism or other extortions and, within a week of the gang's first visit, his business had returned to normal.

The reader should note that there was no violence suggested or displayed in this   scenario.   Every phase of the original act of extortion was executed with politeness and gentle conversation.   There were even the typical acts of respect that can be seen in more normal situations between young adults and their elders in the Vietnamese community. The gang member took great care to suggest only how the owner could comply with their wishes. He also took steps to insure the businessman had an easy way out of the situation. In short, the owner had been presented with the opportunity to avoid a reoccurrence of the six table visit drama by making some food and drink available. While no outrageous demands were ever made, there undoubtedly was the presence of inference and the hint of intimidation.

2.   Extortion - The Honor Guards

Another common crime scenario in 'Little Saigons' involves businesses with two entrances. The gang first targets a business for a hit and then takes up positions at each of its entrances.   As soon as gang members arrive, they position themselves in pairs on each side of all the doorways so that anyone entering must first pass through their review and listen to their comments. Soon, diners begin to turn away at a time when the targetted restaurant would normally have had all of its tables occupied.

Inside, the restaurant owner begins to wonder what has taken place to cause his decline in business. If he looks outside he quickly sees the cause of his dilemna is the gang members, in mismatched 'mod' clothes, who seem to be lounging at his doorway. What the owner may or may not know is that the gang members have been telling potential patrons to steer clear of the eatery since they "expect some trouble inside tonight."

The potential customers heed the warnings and move on down the street.

Finally, unable to endure the lack of customers inside the restaurant, the owner decides to confront his antagonists on the sidewalk. He walks out and is immediately met with polite bows and words in which 'uncle' and 'nephew' are included. The gang members strategy is to extort, without unnecessary coercion, and thus take the tact that what they do is in the best interest of both the restaurant owner and the gang members. They take great care not to make their extortion activity overly zealous as they suggest to the owner that they go inside where they might eat and drink.

Happy to see the problem can be resolved so easily, the restaurant owner quickly accepts the gang's suggestion and invites them inside. Soon, he senses it is to his advantage to ask the gang members to dine and drink with him whenever they are in the area. They accept, of course, and soon the restaurant becomes one of their regular haunts. Again, as in the first scenario, no member of the gang ever offers to pay for food or drink - - nor is it requested of them.

0   Observation

Again, the extortion is successful without obvious threat of violence. The entire transaction is successful because Asian business persons know the reputation of these gangs. They also know that food is cheap and repairing a vandalized business very expensive.

Restaurants, however, are not the only targets of Vietnamese gangs. Any business may be visited by these gangs at anytime. They seldom will stray from the proven approach of politeness and respect knowing full well an inference of terrible consequences can be more frightening than any single act of violence. They take great care in demonstrating that the gang understands the needs of the business person and will often go to great lengths to make it clear they want his business to be successful. In the end, the owner takes the gang members in as partners, at least to the degree they are occasionally fed and given drinks.

Extortion, like blackmail, is a never ending relationship between criminal and victim. Once payment has been made, it is repeated over and over again unless something occurs to break the chain. When one extortion is successful in a community, neighboring businesses begin to get visits by gang members during which their owners are told that payoffs are occurring elsewhere on the street and that it might be wise to participate.

3. Disregard for the Police

East and Southeast Asians are used to doing business without the cover of police protection that is taken so much for granted by most American businessmen. In Asia, police services were not established to 'protect and serve' the community. They were set up to ensure the longevity of rulers and their parties. Asian business-men have long considered paying thugs to move on as just one more cost of doing business - - little more than paying an additional tax.

The vast majority of extortions in the Asian community, whether for goods, services, or money, are never brought to the attention of the police. This lack of reliance upon the police occurs for a wide range of reasons. First, of course, there is fear of eventual retaliation where vandalism, injuries, and even murders may occur involving the business, the owner, and his family. On the other hand, some owners allow extortions to occur through personal indifference or resignation. In between these extremes is an assortment of excuses such as, no confidence in the police, acceptance of extortion as just another cost of doing business, or no belief in or understanding of the criminal justice system.(1)

When, in those rare instances crimes are reported, the subsequent necessity to appear in court and give testimony can be one ordeal too many for the Asian business person to comprehend. Once the court has exposed this business person as the one posing the complaint or giving witness to a crime, he must then return to the Asian community to face both his neighbors and gang members. The concept of appearance in a government function such as a court is foreign to the Vietnamese based mainly on their past experiences in their former homeland where open court testimony is not the practice.(2)

4.   Extortion - The Envelope

An even more subtle way to extort is by 'asking for the envelope.' It begins with the arrival of a group of gang members entering an Asian

Exhibit 1 - The Envelope

business who ask to see the store or restaurant's proprietor. The gang members in their 'mod' clothes stand by quietly as they await the arrival of the businessman. When he arrives, they bow, speak a few words of respect, and then approach him with a question that both he and they fully understand. To the observant but unaware police officer or detective, the actual Vietnamese words would, of course, have no meaning. The paper envelope that passes between the owner and gang members probably would make little sense either.

"Do you have my envelope?" One of the gang might ask the question also by inquiring, "I am here to receive my envelope, Uncle."

In Asian countries it is common practice to give gifts of money in little red envelopes. Traditionally, these envelopes contain 'lucky' money and are given by older persons to children during holidays such as New Year's Day and birthdays. The use of red envelopes has been utilized by some for other than sincere gift giving. In cases of possible bribery, business persons may offer red envelopes to foot patrol officers or investigators as they enter or leave the business place.

0   Observation

All extortion is costly. It is an added financial hardship on the struggling Vietnamese, Chinese, or Korean business persons. It damages the peace and security of the community and undermines what little police credibility and confidence now exists. On the other hand, it is very lucrative for the criminal gangs since each successful extortion provides more goods, services, and money. Even more important and dramatic for the image of the gangs, successful extortion gains them stature and reputation. Extortion enables gangs to establish broad control over communities and to expand their horizons to distant places.

In the few instances where prosecutions are successful, judges seldom render sentences in which maximum jail terms are given. Everyone living in the Asian communities and operating businesses there know that the American justice system seldom holds the criminals fully accountable and no group knows this better than the Asian gangs, themselves. They perform knowing that little can or will be done to them and that few, if any, among the Asian populace will come forward to complain. The lack of follow through by the courts, coupled with the fear of retribution, destroys the will of the businessmen to resist.

The concept of retribution, as perceived by the Vietnamese, is very real. It has been said that Vietnamese will allow hatred to burn in their chests until it is ripe for revenge. Hatred can be borne out of an appearance in court in which the hater has been identified as a responsible in crime. It is no wonder businessmen will endorse the simple providing of food and drink or a small red envelope of money when approached quietly and politely by their gang counterparts.

5. De facto Law Enforcement

There are gangs and times when contact between criminals and businessmen will lack the subtlety and politeness described earlier in this chapter. When this happens, the relationship takes on a slightly different posture. When demands are unreasonable in the sense the gang spokesman asks for too much money, causes damage unnecessarily, or otherwise oversteps what is the norm in such transactions, the intended victim may turn to the community for a satisfactory resolution. This is another Asian cultural phenomenon for in their former homeland it was always acceptable to turn to 'family' for help but never to 'strangers.'

The term, going to the 'stranger,' means turning to government for assistance when there already exists assistance of a kind in the 'family'. Asians have long considered turning to government unacceptable even when the complaining victim had been wronged. To complain publicly is to admit there is disharmony in the Asian community and to bring upon the ethnic enclave shame and disgrace.

This ancient Asian attitude gives rise to the establishment of a de facto law enforcement agency within their community. The establishment and acceptance of such a quasi agency reinforces the separation of the Asian community from its surrounding environment of laws and regulations. In a sense it is policing and controlling. In some ways, it does work to control crime and to keep crime most affecting the Asians from getting out of hand. However, on the down side, it operates without the accepted rules and regulations of the overall community. Obviously, the two systems can not work side-by-side in many countries where the newcomers reside.

6. Terrorism

Although the term, terrorism, is seldom, if ever, used in conjunction with the Vietnamese, it does exist and is an ongoing and continuing problem. Terrorism was defined by the Vice President's Task Force on Combatting Terrorism, as

the unlawful use or threat of violence against persons or property to further political or social objectives. (3)

Terrorism is generally intended to intimidate or coerce a government, individuals, or groups to modify their behavior or policies. The following incidents were brought to the Task Force's attention as examples of Asian terrorist acts.

0   Houston, Texas

On January 24, 1982, a well known Vietnamese publisher, Dam Phong, was murdered in his place of business. The Houston Police, while scouring the scene of his murder inside the Tu Do Magazine publishing plant, uncovered a 'hit list' written in the Vietnamese language. The name at the top of the list was their victim, Dam Phong. The investigators had the list translated into English and it was later used during the government hearings. The translated list is shown in Exhibit 2.

At hearings in October 1984,(4) there was additional testimony from the widow of Dam Phong who reported her husband had been threatened and intimidated into stopping the publication of his Vietnamese language newspaper.(5)

On October 21, 1985, Tien Phong magazine, located in Arlington, Virginia, reported they had received a threating communication. The complainant displayed a printed piece of paper resembling a cash note of a high denomination. Its face contained three words in English and a picture of an oriental building. On its back side was the portrait of an Oriental man and a series of Asian writing. To the unaware, it was play money, something one might expect in a Chinese monoply game. It was no game, however, for its meaning was well known to the Publisher. He saw the note as a final warning of a pending disaster to him which might include his family members, as well. Several years earlier the publisher's home and office was fire bombed supposedly for articles he had printed.

The Vietnamese Party for the Annihiliation
of Communism and for the National Restoration
JUDGEMENT
In compliance with the VPACNR minutes of the meeting dated April 30, 1982, the
following judgement was made;

. . . .

0   DAM PHONG, Publisher of the Tu Do Magazine, Houston, Texas

0   NGUYEN THANH HOANG, Publisher of the Van Nghe Tien Phong
Magazine, Arlington, Virginia

0   LE TRIET, aka TU RUA, Editor of the Van Nghe Tien Phong
Magazine

0   LE MINH TRUC, aka TO VAN, Publisher of the Thuc Tihh
Magazine of California

0   PHAM THU TRUCO, aka VIET DINH PHUONG, Publisher of the
Trang Den Magazine of California

---

are the most dangerous Vietnamese traitors: They have received directives and money from the Vietnamese Central Committee through Overseas Intelligence Operations "RED ROSE" campaign. Their purposes are as follows:

0   To create disagreement, resentment, separation, and suspicion among the Vietnamese communities overseas.

0   To sabotage missions being carried out by various forces, religious   groups, and Nationalist Vietnamese Communities overseas.

0   To sabotage missions being carried out by various National   Restoration and Resistance Movements.

Exhibit 2 - Threatening Communication

On occasion, targetted Asian victims are warned of their pending demise by receipt of an envelope containing a written message and some pieces of paper with the appearance of money. The 'money' isn't spendable, however, and is called Hell Bank Notes. For the alive and healthy Asian receiving an envelope containing one or more of the Hell Bank Notes, as was the case with the publisher, it is a direct message the note sender is conveying that he does not wish the receiver well. It is a message of death, instead, and that the often unknown sender plans to assist the victim on his way. The recipient of the note sometimes can adjust his life or change his attitude on a major issue in time to reduce the need for murder. Hell Bank Notes are commonly used in both Chinese and Vietnamese funeral ceremonies during which the notes are burned as offerings to the gods. By burning the paper notes, the burner seeks to aid the departed enter the hereafter as a rich person. The notes are printed in a variety of denominations and are purchased in Asian grocery stores where they are shelved in amongst other funeral and ceremonial items such as incense, joss paper, and joss sticks.

0   Arlington, Virginia

The Arlington Vietnamese language magazine, Tien Phong, received both a letter and three Hell Bank Notes in October, 1985, presumably because its publisher had been singled out as working for the communists. The letter, translated by first one Vietnamese and then verified in a second encounter with another interpreter, reads as shown in Exhibit 4.

The interpreter analyzed Dai Nam's writings and came up with a great number of rather startling observations of which a few are described here. First, he assumed the writer was an extremist or right winger and from the former South Vietnam. Next, by using the words, brass candies, he understood the writer was referring to bullets since brass candies is Vietnamese slang for projectiles from firearms. The reference to eating sorghum and canned corn in the third sentence was the writer's way of describing that poor Vietnamese eat sorghum and canned corn is found only in

Exhibit 3 - Example of Hell Bank Note

I will fuck your mother you Tien Phong.

I will give all of you to eat brass candies.

You are a mercenary soldier for the Americans.

The Vietnamese people will eat sorghum and canned corn.

I give you these offerings before.

Accept this money to look for Ho, the dead dog.

Signed: Dai Nam

Exhibit 4 - Translated Letter

the United States. Its true implication was not known to either interpreters.

The note in the fourth line may have been added to imply the subject of the threat cannot hide since the enemies of Ho Chi Minh are everywhere. In writing the fifth line, the writer was implying he had attempted at least once before to reach the victim and would try again in the future. By mentioning the Hell Bank Notes the writer was emphasizing that death was near and that the recipient would soon be face-to-face with Ho.

0   Maryland

On August 6, 1987, a Vietnamese man was in his bathroom when two shots were fired through his window. One struck his shoulder before he dropped from view of the window to avoid further shots. During the investigation that followed, the victim claimed he did not know why he was shot at or why his home had been selected in the first place. Later, he admitted the shooting may have been the work of a Vietnamese political group called the 'Action Squad.'

Some investigators believe the so-called 'Action Squad' may be something new in the United States and has the right wing goal of striking out against persons who are too left politically, are leaders in the community, or voices in the press. No proof has surfaced, as yet, to make the 'Action Squad' a reality. The shooting is still under investigation since no leads have developed nor has anyone come forward with facts about the 'Squad.'(6)

0   California

In August, 1987, a well known publisher of a Vietnamese language newspaper in Westminster, California was found dead inside his arsoned residence. Investigators sought out the motive for the killing thinking, at first, it might have been a foiled burglary or a resisted robbery. No evidence of either crime was ever substantiated. It is now believed that the publisher was murdered gangland style and his home set on fire to cover up the crime.(7)

These incidents are not the only examples of such criminal activity. These are merely highlight cases to show terrorist activities, as defined by the Vice President's Task Force on Combatting Terrorism, and Asian criminals are a continuing and ongoing matter in communities wherever Asians have settled.

7. Armed Robberies

The most popular targets for robberies in Asian communities are the jewelry stores. The targets are plentiful as there seems to be an inordinate high number of the stores when compared with jewelry stores operated by non-Asians in the same community.

The Vietnamese jewelry stores all have a large and expensive inventory of precious stones and 24 carat gold along with the typical displays of 18 and 14 carat gold, as well. Seldom does one find an Asian store equipped with buzzers to alert the operators of entry from either the rear or front entrances. Few have installed electronic alarm systems but rely on watchful family members to protect them from thefts, robberies, and the like.

The most common robbery method used by Asian criminals, when attacking jewelry stores, is to storm inside quickly and take immediate control over both the employees and patrons. Once inside, one of the three or four robbers removes a hammer from his clothing and smashes the glass case displays. While his compatriates stand guard, he scoops up the desired 24 carat gold and the precious stones. He throws them in a bag or valise and leads the way out of the store. The whole robbery takes only minutes to execute and by the time the victims have recovered from their fear, the shock of the threats, and broken glass, the robbers are in their car and far from the jewelry store.

It is interesting to note that few robbers take anything more than the high carat gold and precious stones. They leave behind cash, checks, and other items that would be normal 'take' for many non-Asian robbers in similar situations.

0   Observation

Seldom do the robbers harm either the patrons or the employees. Most robbers are unknown to their victims and are thus believed to be travellers from other towns. In the situations where apprehensions have been made the robbers have been found to be young (in their late teens), well armed, very nervous, and excited.

8. Home Invasion Robberies

All home invasion robberies should be carefully studied before reporting them as one crime or another. Some, obviously, are very real as in the recent several home robberies reported in California. In these cases, the eight suspects had been travelling up and down the state striking the homes of Asians for what the homes contained in the way of precious jewels, gold, and other items of value. Police had been looking for them for a long time and had given them the title, 'The L.A. Boys.'(8)

When arrested, they had just completed two home invasion robberies and had gone into hiding in an apartment complex before heading out again. Among their crimes were car theft, burglary, conspiracy, and robbery. Investigators determined that the eight men had no permanent addresses and lived off crime as they travelled from town to town.

Some home invasion robberies, however, are not what they first seem. One common scenario has it occurring during a birthday party for a little boy or girl when several young men gain entry by brandishing guns and knives. They promptly rob all the guests of their cash, jewels, and gold and then flee. When the police arrive, they are told the combined losses of ten guests is in the estimated range of $10,000 to $20,000. To add to the suspicious nature of the claimed home invasion robbery is the fact there are only a few children on view in the home area. Experience has shown that more than likely a high stakes gambling game had been going on and was simply robbed by persons who had heard about the game and were waiting for such an opportunity to occur.

It is possible that the robbery was staged by one of the participants or by the organizer himself since it is a rarity when such games are held very often in one place. The chances of a robber hitting the game at the precise right moment are slim at best. Investigators should be mindful of these other elements when attempting to record a home invasion robbery. A home invasion robbery is generally not a random target. It is a high risk venture similar to robbing a jewelry store. Just as the rewards of a successful jewelry store make the risk worthwhile so, too, are the rewards equally high in a home invasion robbery.

9. Residential Burglaries

It is a cultural tradition for Asians to convert currency into gold and precious gems. They prefer to keep these valuables in their homes rather than make the use of banking services.(9) These two simple, but well known facts, make nearly every Asian residence a high potential for burglary. Precious stones such as diamonds, rubies, and jade are not bulky and are relatively easy to store out of sight. The gold, in the form of taels is even easier to hide because of its shape and small size.(10)

Vietnamese burglars choose their targets much the same as other non-Asian burglars. If they want a video player or camera, they go where they can expect to find such devices. If they want gold and jewels, they also know full well where they are likely to find gold and jewels in abundance. When they are after large stakes, they may also go to the trouble to isolate one business person, from among several, as having the highest potential for hoarding gold and precious stones in a hiding place in his home. Once they have located his residence, following a period of staking the business person out between his shop and his home, then they devise the best time for their attack. If at all possible, they will attempt to strike when the business person and his family are away from the residence.

A few Vietnamese burglars have admitted to making their selection simply by looking up Vietnamese in the local phone book.

In some crime situations, what starts out to be a plain and simple daytime residential burglary evolves quickly into an abduction and robbery. In many Asian families both husband and wife work full time away from their home. When they have children, they may be cared for by some older relative or hired baby sitter. The fact that the children and the sitter may be home mid-day may catch the burglars by surprise. When this occurs, they normally tie up the sitter and, in some cases, have been known to abuse and assault whomever may be present. Injuries and murders occur often enough that home burglaries are greatly feared by many in the Asian community.(11)

When burglaries are reported to the police, it is interesting to read the list of lost property. Usually there is very little cash missing but instead, thousands of dollars worth of jewelry, precious stones, and gold taels. It is obvious there must exist an outlet for these expensive items since only a portion of them can be retained by the burglars and another small segment of them sold directly on the street. Many investigators, specializing in Asian crimes, feel there are a number of fencing operators to whom the criminals go for orders and to whom they deliver and receive payment.

10. Narcotics Trafficking and Use

Asian involvement in the narcotics business is not new. They have been and are currently involved in every phase of the narcotics industry including manufacturing, refining, smuggling, selling, and using. There is little reason to expect the future will hold anything different regarding narcotics and Asian involvement.

According to testimony at the Hearings before the Permanent Subcommittee on Investigations, September 24, 1986, between 20 and 25 percent of the heroin available in New York City was from Southeast Asia and is controlled by Asian traffickers.(12)   A recent Washinton Post story reported Burma has increased its opium production and some Lao opium is believed now entering the international market through ports in Vietnam.   The report added that Thailand was also experiencing significant growth, in the export trade, of a particularly potent and highly sought after form of marijuana.(13)

0   Observation

Narcotics usage by Asians is virtually the same as for non-Asian users. Every drug that can be acquired is consumed from marijuana to heroin.   They also suffer the same results such as addiction, overdoses, shakedowns, thefts, and the associated violence that comes with being involved in this crime area.(14)   Many are active traffickers and many have been arrested and imprisoned for their offenses.(15) Information from sources on the street points out that Vietnamese are also part of intrastate networks especially along the east coast of the United States.(16)   Two examples of their deep involvement are the following:

The U.S. Drug Enforcement Agency developed a case in Virginia in which a Chinese-Vietnamese man sold heroin to an Agency undercover non-Asian agent. The seller was later convicted and sent to prison. Recently he was released having served his time without ever having identified his fellow traffickers. Confidential sources state that his original partners are also Chinese-Vietnamese, are deeply invested in a Virginia restaurant business, and have intact narcotic connections in New York.

Law Enforcement authorities in New Orleans, Louisana stated they have evidence of a relationship between local traditional organized groups and Southeast Asians distributing cocaine and marijuana in their state.(17)

11. Asian Gambling

In the early 1980's Arlington Virginia vice squad executed a search warrant to obtain gambling records and gambling paraphenalia from a Thai's residence. The search resulted in the seizure of very specific and detailed records of a gambling operation that covered many of the major sports in the United States. It was interesting to note that this illegal gambling operation followed closely the rules of other Asian gambling in that it was limited to Thai players and had Thai management.(18) No one was allowed inside its doors during play unless they were Thai and well known to the operators. The gambling operation might still be functioning had it not been for an anonymous tip to local police.

In the Fall of 1984, following a three month investigation into gambling in 'Little Saigon' of Arlington, Virginia, officers were successful in identifying and prosecuting both the game's primary operator and a number of her agents, as well. Books and notes were seized and from them came an elaborate network of crime activity that linked the operator and her gambling to a number of residences and business outlets in several distant locations. An analysis of her cash flow showed she was netting about $100,000 per week and had been doing so for several years.

The female operator had taken great care not to play her gambling games in only one place and to limit her gamblers to only known Vietnamese. She regularly operated out of various residences in Virginia and Washington, D.C. and out of four businesses, as well. Games were high stake with amounts of $5,000 to $20,000 on display most of the time. A number of her players travelled great distances with some addresses in Florida and Louisiana. She offered them the games of blackjack, twenty-one, poker, other card, dice options, and sport betting.

Not all Asian gambling dens are as organized as the ones described above. Some simply get started in the backrooms of Asian businesses where they are brought together when a few people are available with money and who want to play. Many Chinese restaurants permit, if not actually operate, gambling games in their back rooms and kitchens after regular business hours. Often, the players will be the employees of the restaurants with some invited guests included. Nearly always, the players are Asians and well known to the group as a whole. Bets are large as in the floating or rotating gambling games described earlier and the cash in hand is in the thousands of dollars.

Most Asians in the community know which of the Chinese restaurants host gambling and that large bets are made in them. Because of this general knowledge, the kitchens and backrooms of these restaurants make tempting targets for Asian robbers.(19)

Often it is has been said that ". . . gambling is part of the Chinese or Asian culture." It is true the Chinese, in particular, enjoy gambling and have been known to bet practically anything they possess having some value. But this in no way either mitigates or excuses the illegal aspects of gambling. A friendly wager or poker game among friends is one thing. However, a well organized gambling organization grossing $100,000 per week is quite another.(20) It goes well beyond the cultural practices argument when the cash flow from gambling is directed toward other crimes, attracts criminals from other areas, buys votes, avoids taxes, and generally gives the operator an unfair purchasing advantage over the legitimate business persons.

13. Prostitution

A recent United States Immigration and Naturalization Service report sums up Korean prostitution as follows: "A Korean Organized Crime Syndicate known as the KK or KTA (Korean Tourist Association) is involved in procuring Korean females to work as prostitutes both in Korea and in the United States. The most common method of gaining entry into the United States for these females is to

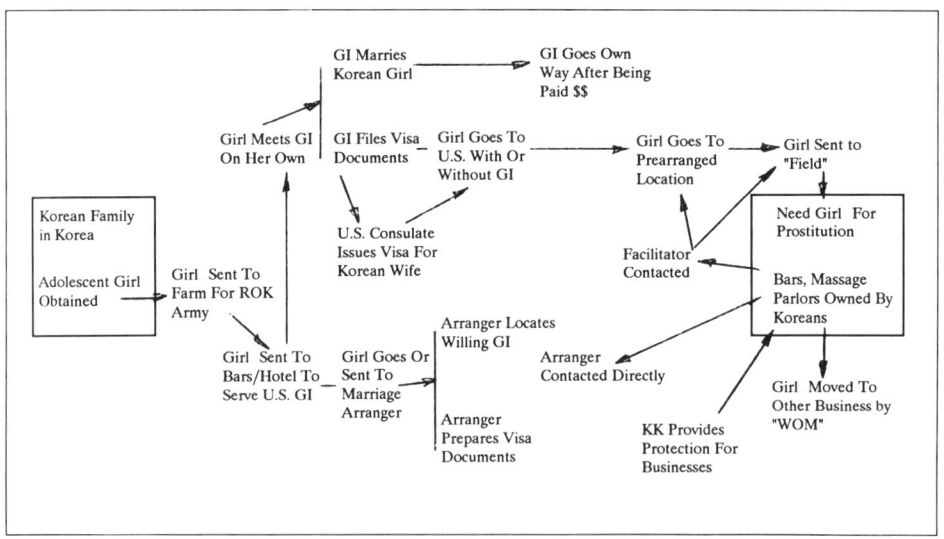

Exhibit 5 - Korean Marriage Fraud and Prostitution Scheme

arrange a 'sham' marriage between them and U.S. servicemen stationed in Korea. Once married, the new wives enter the country as immigrants. The KK, while usually not in direct control of the prostitution activities in America, maintains close association with Koreans involved in the operation of the front businessses. The KK provides protection services to some Korean businesses which conduct prostitution activities in the United States." An event chart reflecting KK involvement in Korean marriage fraud and prostitution schemes is shown in Exhibit 5.

0   Korean Activity

In April 1986, there were a series of search and arrest warrants executed across the United States which involved a prostitution operation that spanned four locations: Nationalist China; San Francisco, California; Houston, Texas; and New York City, New York.(23)

0   Vietnamese Activity

Undercover operatives in the Washington, D.C. area report that Vietnamese criminals are engaging in prostitution enterprises on a relatively large scale. The gang's girls travel, in groups of four girls, with each going from one Vietnamese community to the next. They are known to criss-cross the entire nation as part of their modus operandi. Each of the groups usually consist of four girls; three Vietnamese and one caucasian. They stay in rented apartments for about six weeks before a group is moved to another Asian community. A second group of four girls may arrive shortly after their counterparts have moved on and take up residence in a rented apartment near where the first operation was located. No investigator has yet uncovered proof of a national organization dictating the make up of the Vietnamese foursomes, where they will go, where they will stay, or other organizational details. Several officers have speculated the groups may still be independent and only following the path of least resistance.

0   Observation

For a variety of reasons, both Korean and Vietnamese prostitution rings are difficult to infiltrate. One major obstacle with the Vietnamese operations is the fact they stay in one place only a short period of time before moving their entire cadre of prostitutes elsewhere. A second law enforcement problem is the fact that both the Koreans and Vietnamese tend to provide their sexual services only to Asians. Little can be composed in the form of investigations without some problem occurring either from within the prostitute circles or from the people they serve. The following suggestions and indicators are offered here to guide future investigations into Asian prostitution crime.

0   Develop local street sources who can provide intelligence about prostitution services in the community and about those due to arrive.

0   Seek out the prostitute that seems the least enthusiastic about her work and propose a plan for her safe exit in return for information.

0   Utilize an Asian officer from a neighboring community to make himself available for the gang's sexual services.

0   Follow up on calls from the public regarding Asian prostitutes working out of rented apartments.

0   Encourage patrol officers to report sightings of out-of-town cars occupied by four girls; three Asian and one Caucasian.

0   Utilize tips from Asian crime 'competitors' who want to report presence of prostitutes.

14.   Larcenies

The most common object of larceny for Asians, in general, is the automobile. Law enforcement officers state unequivocally that the Datsun and Toyota makes are by far the most popular over all other makes. What makes them most appealing is the fact they are easily unlocked, easily started, and easy to drive. Investigators have found Asian car thieves use little more than blank keys shaved to points or tiny wires taken from windshield wiper blades to open doors and start ignitions. Both techniques are fast and reliable. If stopped and shaken down by investigators, the disposal of the shaved key or the wiper wire is a simple thing to accomplish.

In New Orleans, Louisiana, Asian criminals came up with yet another scheme to use their Datsuns and Toyotas for making easy money. First, they brought their own personal car in and left it with the Asian garage owner where their car was quickly torched and otherwise dismantled and its parts placed on shelves for sale. They then located and stole a car of a similar make, doors, and year and used their personal registration, tags, and VIN number to operate their new find safely on the street. This gave gang members quick cash for the parts from their former car and a car in better condition to drive.

Sometimes, theft occurs because the item desired is there for the taking - - or so some thieves are led to believe. In 1985, one Vietnamese thief on the east coast was arrested and in his car was found a flashlight with a law enforcement officer's name on it. It had been stolen several months earlier when an unidentified person broke into a police car in an unsuccessful attempt to remove the shot gun.

In the mid-1980s police officers in a city in the east uncovered a bad check scheme and made arrests of several Vietnamese males. After many interviews of witnessess and interrogations of the arrestees, the investigators found the following modus operandi behind their crimes. First, they struck only the parking areas of large non-Asian apartment complexes where they broke into cars containing identification papers, blank checks, and credit cards. Second, they tried to pass the checks and use the cards even though the checks and credit cards were made out to non-Asians. At the time of the arrests, officers found one arrestee with six personal identifications in an envelope and none of whom were Asian. The envelope was stamped and addressed to a Vietnamese in Oklahoma.

Several of these examples demonstrate that Asian criminals are not always clever or intelligent when planning and executing their crimes. The latter example shows, too, that they are more than willing to step out of the Asian community and commit crimes elsewhere should the idea and the opportunity arise.

15. Summary

There is nothing unusual about the types of crimes as described in this Chapter that make them stand out from what have been committed by other ethnic groups. But, when the whole picture is examined, one can see some major myths being eliminated. The following has been found to be true:

- 0   Asian groups of differing ethnic backgrounds are working together
- 0   Asian gangs will commit crimes against non-Asians
- 0   Asian criminals will team with non-Asians to commit crimes

Asians can no longer be thought of as all being law abiding citizens as they were once portrayed. No longer will court, jail, and prison statistics be devoid of data relative to their crime involvement. In the recent past, criminal behavior by Asians was treated as a family problem, certainly nothing more than an Asian community problem, which could and would be controlled and corrected by the people within the community. Today, however, unlike the past, Asian criminals are more mobile, lack family ties and tight community controls, and are motivated by past events to take what they wish and kill if they must. The worst is yet to be seen as they organize and get more deeply committed to the crimes of their choice. Soon, as some Asian experts now believe, Asian criminals will join and even form confederations with non-Asians. They will probably replace the traditional Mafia and other criminal groups that America and the rest of the free world has faced and feared for so long.

Notes   (1)   The lack of understanding of the American Criminal Justice System is not unique to Asians.   There are many native-born persons who do not fathom it, as well.

(2)   <u>Author</u>: As it has been explained to me by former police officers and other officials of South Vietnam, victims of crimes report them to the police chief or magistrate who decides if the crime will be investigated and prosecuted.   When arrests were made and suspects brought to trial, only the investigator testifies and he does this on behalf of the victim.   This eliminates the need for the victim and the accused to face one another.

(3)   Public Report of the Vice President's Task Force in Combatting Terrorism, February 1986, <u>The Nature of Terrorism</u>, p. 1.

(4)   President's Commission on Organized Crime, Record of Hearing III, October 23-25, 1984, <u>Organized Crime of Asian Origin</u>, pp. 347-361.

(5)   Ibid., pp. 362-376.

(6)   Information provided through the courtesy of the Montgomery County Police Department, Montgomery County, Maryland.

(7)   Information provided through the courtesy of the Westminster Police

Notes   Department, Westminster, California. At this writing there have been no
arrests made.

(8) Sacramento Bee Newspaper, 8 Held In Gang Attacks On 2 Sacramento
Families, 12-16-87, p. B4.   On April 19, 1988, robber Quoc Nguyen Bao
Cong, 19, pleaded guilty in Superior Court to the armed robberies of two
Sacramento area Vietnamese families. Cong was sentenced to eight years
in California's penal system. Cong's co-defendent, Thien Ngoc Vo, also
19, had not been sentenced at the time of this writing.

(9) Historically the banks of Korea, China, and Vietnam have always been
operated in a loose manner. They have been manipulated by their owners
and the government. Area citizens found one had to convert currency into
gold and precious stones to beat inflation. Thus the habit of avoiding banks
and storing valuables at home has long been established.

(10) A tael is a standard Chinese measurement. A packaged tael measures
3 and 3/4 inch by 1 and 1/2 inch and weighs 1 troy ounce. It is 24 carat with
a constant value of what the daily market dictates.

(11) Whether these killings are accidental or intentional is irrelevant as far
as law enforcement, the Asian community, the victim, and the victim's
family are concerned.

(12) From testimony given by Robert Stutman, Special Agent in Charge,
New York Field Division, Drug Enforcement Administration, during the
Emerging Criminal Groups Hearings before the Permanent Subcommit-
tee on Investigations, September 24, 1986, Report of Hearings, p. 67.

(13) Washington Post, Drugs are Major Industry in Thailand, Laos, and

Notes   <u>Burma</u>, March 28, 1987.

(14) <u>Author</u>: On a Sunday afternoon during September, 1987, I spoke with a 17 year old Vietnamese male who, along with several other friends, had been charged with the first degree murder of an adult black man earlier in the day. The shooting death came as a result of an attempted drug rip-off. In response to my question about his drug use he responded, "I only smoke boat." He further told me 'boat' wasn't drugs or dope as only heroin and opium fit that description.

(15)   Information provided through the courtesy of the Criminal Intelligence Unit, Boston Police Department, Boston, Massachusetts.

(16)   In August, 1985, in Falls Church, Virginia there was a stabbing between two Vietnamese. The investigation revealed the victim to be from the New York City area and to be an associate of the Flying Dragons. The knife fight had been over the issue of cocaine distribution in the Metropolitan Washington, D.C. area.

(17)   From the testimony at the President's Commission on Organized Crime, <u>Record of Hearings III</u>, p. 488.

(18)   The records were so good that they are now being used for demonstration purposes at the Federal Bureau of Investigation's school on gambling.

(19)   Southern Florida had two cases in which Asian restaurants were robbed in the early morning hours long after the restaurants had been closed for business. To explain why so many people were present at the time of one of the robberies, one of the Chinese said they had been

Notes   conducting a Chinese Businessman's Association meeting.

(20) A high ranking Department of Defense official wrote to the woman's probation officer on her behalf. He wrote: "I would suggest the trangressions . . . be viewed in a cultural context."

(21) Record of Emerging Criminal Groups Hearings before the Permanent Subcommittee on Investigations, September 24, 1986, pp. 63-64.

CHAPTER FOUR

Not all Asian crime is of the rob and grab kind. In many situations the criminals are cunning, long range in their planning, and have great skills and knowledge in their crime field. This chapter outlines a few of their more sophisticated crimes. The reader will soon see that these operations are set in motion and continually operated by educated professionals and successful business persons. These are the same persons who, for all intents and purposes, should be using their higher educations and positions to benefit those around them. Instead, a few of the educated and well positioned have chosen to use their minds and positions to operate enterprises that exploit their people and engage them in their criminal activities.

1. Distribution of Controlled Substances

In just about any issue of a Vietnamese language newspaper there can be found advertisements for and by Vietnamese owned and operated pharmacies. Invariably, these advertisements will contain statements indicating customers can purchase without prescription and for shipment to Vietnam such items as Ampicillin, Tetramycin and Streptomycin. All three items are sorely needed in Vietnam where the drugs are nearly impossible to obtain and in this country they are protected by laws requiring dissemination by prescription only. See the newspaper advertisement in Exhibit 1.

In addition to the newspaper advertisement, the Vietnamese customer may review a printed list of other pharmaceutical supplies prominantly displayed in an area near the pharmacist. Many of the listed items, just as those named in the advertisement, require prescriptions in order to be purchased. Many Vietnamese pharmacies sell prescription only items, in large quantities, to any Vietnamese who places an order and and has the money to purchase them.

PHARMACY

* Bán các loại Âu Dược theo toa Bác Sĩ, hướng dẫn cách dùng thuốc rõ ràng bằng tiếng Việt.

* Nhận Medicaid và các loại bảo hiểm, và miễn phí cho thuốc OTC và các phụ thu.

* Dược Sĩ VN tốt nghiệp tại Hoa Kỳ hướng dẫn tận tình.

* Bán tất cả các thuốc để gởi về VN mà không cần phải có toa như là TRỤ SINH thuốc đau bao tử, huyết áp cao, suy tim, thuốc lao (Ampicillin Tetracyclin Streptomycin, Lincocin)

* Co bán các oại thuớc của Phap như là Sulfarlem, Chophytol, Pharmaton. Apiserum v.v...

* Có bán những thùng thuốc đặc biệt để gởi về VN gồm có các loại thuốc thông dụng ở thị trường VN bán được giá cao.

Giờ mở cửa:
Thứ Hai - Thứ Bảy: 10:00 am - 7:00 pm
Chủ Nhật: 10:00 am - 2:00 pm

Exhibit 1 - U.S. Newspaper Advertisement (Edited)

A recently concluded joint investigation in one east coast state resulted in the arrest and conviction of a Vietnamese pharmacist for distribution of controlled substances.(1) The pharmacist who owned and operated the pharmacy in a Vietnamese shopping mall had, on several occasions, sold to undercover officers hundreds of dollars of medicines which the officer ordered off the list of available items for sale. The medicines were clearly marked, *U.S. Federal law prohibits dispensing without prescription*. There was no effort made by the pharmacist to act as a distributor. He had considered the transaction to be nothing more than a standard retail sale. It is noted here that the reason for the Vietnamese activities with pharmaceuticals is their value on the black market in Vietnam. See the partial pharmacy list in Exhibit 2.

Vietnamese pharmacists have no corner on the distribution of controlled substances. Local Asian stores will sometimes branch out from their professed business of groceries or artifacts and begin advertising the sale of certain drugs known to be of high interest to their Vietnamese customers. The advertisements are most often limited to store windows, rather than newspapers or flyers, but their drawing power is obvious and their clients are specifically focussed on the Asian population. They are always composed in the ethnic language of the anticipated client group. One such advertisement initiated an investigation which resulted in the arrest of a non-pharmacist store owner and the seizure of a large quantity of his prescription medicines. See the newspaper clipping in Exhibit 1.

The arrestee began as a retailer of controlled substances and, in some cases, acted as a distributor since he packaged and sent controlled substances to designated recipients in Vietnam.

```
TRU SINH

Ampicillin    250mg--100v--$12.00
Ampicillin    500mg--100v--$17.00
Erythromycin250mg--100v--$15.00
Erythromycin500mg--100v--$24.00
Tetracyclin 250mg--100v--$10.00
Tetracyclin 500mg--100v--$13.00
Tifomycin     250mg--100v--$23.00
Lincocin      500mg-- 24v--$24.00
Penicillin  250mg--100v--$10.00
Penicillin  500mg--100v--$13.00
Lincocin chich------2cc--$ 8.00
Lincocin chich-----10cc--$24.00

CAN CUM SO MUI HO

Ornade generic--100v--$ 9.00
Dimacol---------100v--$14.00
Naldecon--------100v--$13.00
Purebron--------100v--$13.00
THUOC CAM SAU

Syckavite-------100v--$13.00

DAU BA DAY, DAU BUNG

Bentyl generic--100v--$ 8.00
Tagamet 300mg---100v--$44.00
Zantac 150mg----60v--$64.00

DAU GAN BO GAN

Chophytol------180v--$10.00
Liver extract--30cc--$14.00

LOI TIEU

Lasix 20mg generic--100v--$10.00
Dyazide-----------100v--$29.00
HCTZ 25mg---------100v--$ 9.00

HUYET AP CAO

Aldomet 250mg------100v--$29.00
Aldomet generic----100v--$19.00
Lopressor 100mg----100v--$48.00

PHO MAT

Decadron----------10--$13.00
Dexamethasone-----10--$ 9.00
Garamycin---------10--$ 9.00
Blephamide-------10--$13.00
```

Exhibit - 2 - Pharmacy List

2. Importation of Controlled Substances

Investigators must always question how it is the drugs are available since they are highly controlled and, for all purposes, under strict record keeping and enforcement. Some might speculate the Asian market people must be visiting Mexico or some other foreign country for their source of the prescription drugs. The evidence shows it arrives in much more legitimate form - - through the U.S. mails. One known origin is certain drug manufacturers in France. Many federal law enforcement agencies now have extensive case files showing large quantities of controlled substances being shipped to addresses of Vietnamese businesses.(2)

TRU SINH

Antibiotics   Ampicillin
Ampi . . .   Terra . . .
Tetracyclin (?) Peni . . . Penicillin

Order Khong Can Nhanh
Order without prescription Inexpensive and fast delivery to BN

Re Va Ve Vn Nhanh

Exhibit 3 - Window Display, Vietnamese Store

Many of the pharmaceuticals seized by one east coast police agency from a Vietnamese owned business in 1984 were of French origin.(3) In the same year, U.S. Customs also seized a significant quantity of valium from France which bore the address of a Vietnamese outlet in the United States.

In 1985, the Drug Enforcement Administration in Kansas City, Missouri worked a nationwide case involving valium coming from France which had been distributed in large quantities in both Vietnamese and non-Vietnamese communities.

Obviously, many controlled drugs continue to slip through the borders of the nation while being hand-carried, by clever packaging and labeling, or by other techiques. The Asian pharmacies and stores continue to make it available even though an occasional arrest is made or interception of drugs is successful. It is also important to remember that the vast majority of Asians whether they are Chinese, Korean, Laotian, Vietnamese, etc., do not want drugs in their community in any form unless it is acquired in accordance with the law.

3. Frauds

Many Asians turn to fraud because it is simple to do, of low risk, and highly lucrative. They seem to know that police will not spend time working on anything but major crime cases and that insurance companies and government regulatory agencies are forced to abandon all but the most important cases because of limited resources and other priorities. Asian fraud involvement includes employment and welfare, auto accident claims, property loss, medical insurance, and accidents involving personal injury. Their fraudulent claims are only as limited as their imaginations.

Certainly, many of the involved Asian criminals must see America and the other countries, in which they have settled, as poorly policed and uncoordinated when compared with where they once lived. Many of them have perceptions that money is available without working and that their new homeland is eager to make money and assistance available to them without much question.

0   Insurance Companies

Private insurance companies are being victimized in great numbers and with substantial losses because of Asian criminals.(4) Although these same companies seldom document anything about these losses, reliable and confidential Vietnamese sources have personally displayed overstated bills which they say were submitted by their doctors to insurance companies. These bills reflected services which were never provided and when payments were returned to the doctors, the monies were divided between the doctors and their patients.

Confidential sources also allude to numerous insurance related schemes involving Vietnamese owned automobile repair shops wherein estimates and repairs are supposedly generated for the sole purpose of collecting on the make believe damages.

Falsified injury claims are also submitted through cooperating Asian and non-Asian attorneys. The insurance agencies refuse to offer figures when asked for estimates of losses due to fraudulent claims offered by Asian criminals. Although they do not give reasons for refusing to share this information, if it is available, many outside the industry believe they are withholding out of fear they will tarnish their image as a stable industry. The loss is high, perhaps in the millions of dollars each year and the losses are passed on to the general public as the cost of doing business. The losses are not limited to insurance companies, however, since city, county, state, and national governments are also victims of these and other fraudulent crimes on perhaps a yet bigger scale.

Government records that separate Asian fraud crime from non-Asian are seldom maintained making it nearly impossible to determine the true size of the community and national problem.

Many Vietnamese claim it is common knowledge in their community that there is major abuse of medicaid and social services. Many Asians are both concerned and outraged by the government's laissez faire attitude toward these crimes.

One confidential source was so upset he wrote a number of letters to elected officials and to the press in which he complained about Vietnamese fraud activities.(5) Some of the replies he received were ludicrous. All showed a blatant lack of sensitivity for the crime problem. One such reply received by the Vietnamese source from a member of the U.S. Congress is shown in Exhibit 4.

Congress of the United States
House of Representatives
Washington, DC 20515

18 December, 1985

Your letter regarding the Vietnamese medical community has been brought to my attention. I can certainly appreciate your concerns in this matter. At this time I have contacted the Office of the Attorney General to request the current status of this matter and when further action may be expected. Rest assured that I will be back in touch with you as soon as information is forthcoming.

Sincerely, Member of Congress

Exhibit 4 - Congressional Response

4. Currency Transfers

In 1984 there was a Senate hearing regarding Vietnamese currency transfers. At this hearing there was expert testimony to the effect that millions of U.S. dollars were being sent abroad to relatives in Vietnam and that only a small portion of the cash was reaching the intended recipients. The larger share, the experts said, was taken in by the Socialist Republic of Vietnam Government.(6)

The U.S. Foreign Assets Control Act provides and allows for a minimal amount of money to be sent to individuals in Vietnam. However, the allegations at the time of the hearings, which are still repeated today, are monies in great excess of the allowed amounts are being sent to Vietnam.(7)

This excessive and illegal amount of money transfers must be executed in a most secret manner. It is believed the persons effecting the transfers utilize commercial Telex machines and are connected to some form of an international organization.

Knowledgable persons in federal law enforcement and in the world of commerce claim the existing money transfers between the United States and Vietnam require a strong linkage from one end of the system to the other. They know it takes a strong working relationship between business points in the United States and official receivers in Vietnam. Everyone believes such a system does exist but exactly how it works has yet to be determined. No one inside the American Vietnamese community with the overall knowledge of the system has come forward with the details.

5. Exploitation

Exploitation of Asians could be construed as another form of extortion. Certain political activists in the Vietnamese communities use the nationalistic ideals of getting the Vietnam homeland back from the communists for collecting large amounts of money. Much of the collected money, it is believed, does not go toward the building of a war chest but, instead, toward the enrichment of the exploiters.

Another commonly planned activity in the Asian community is exploiting any real or imagined relationships with authority figures such as, city managers, politicians, and police officials. The Asians are very aware of the vanity of public officials and use this failing to their advantage. A classic example is arranging to have a picture taken with the Asian businessman standing beside the official. Once framed, the businessman displays it in a prominent place where all his Asian neighbors, associates, and relatives are sure to take full account. The inference taken from the picture rings clear in the minds of the Asian community: the government official is in the businessman's 'hip pocket' or is his 'protector.' It also gives the Asian in the picture a certain amount of 'face' or prestige.

Occasionally, an Asian businessman has decided not to donate to a cause, for one reason or another, and says 'no' to the requestor. When this happens, he is subject to charges of being a communist sympathizer whether true or not. Since the vast majority of Vietnamese are anti-communist, this places him in a poor business and social position which he will find unacceptable in short order.

6. Kickbacks

These are nothing new in today's politico-economic life. However, there are two scams going on in the Vietnamese community which have not been readily reported to the non-Asian community. Both have to do with real estate. One involves a Vietnamese buyer who shops around the various Vietnamese real estate agents until he locates the agent willing to rebate the highest amount of his sales commission to the buyer. This scheme relies upon the eagerness of the Vietnamese salesperson to sell slow moving property.

The second scheme requires the buyer to give the salesman all of the required down payment money, up front, for a property. The salesman is asked to register the property in the salesman's name so that the buyer can remain on government assistance and perhaps keep his personal wealth hidden from both his neighbors and government officials. The buyer is then told the property will become his when the last of the monthly payments has been made to the salesman. The question must eventually arise over property ownership when the last payment has been made by the buyer and the property remains in the salesman's name. The scheme seems to work because the salesman knows the motive behind the arrangement. Vietnamese real estate agents and community leaders state the two schemes are very much a part of Asian community life and no one affected by them is complaining to government officials.(8)

7. Asset Hiding

The Vietnamese and other Asians make use of gold, diamonds, and other precious stones as a trading commodity thereby creating their own underground currency. With this use of gold in place of currency they are able to avoid developing paper trails and, in so doing, they are able to evade taxes. In some cases, those who are on some sort of welfare subsistence are employed by fellow Vietnamese who pay them 'under the table.'   While building up their 'fortune,' in this manner, they continue to receive government subsistence.

With these two cash payments, under the table pay and government subsistence, the recipients convert their cash to gold.   When they have accumulated enough assets, they remove the gold from hiding and buy their own businesses. The hiding of assets is one reason there is a great disparity in reporting of crime in Asian communities.   Many have found it is better to remain quiet, to start over, than to bring the government and its police into thefts, burglaries, and robberies. When police arrive, they ask questions and the questions can lead to discoveries of illegal gambling, prostitution, drug trafficking, evasion of taxes, unlawful government assistance, and many other crimes.(9)   To bring in the police can also attract the wrath of Asian gangs and the demise of the complainer's business and social position, as well.

The matter of money laundering should be addressed in any commentary concerning asset hiding. It will suffice to briefly note here that the same money laundering methods apply with Asians as they do with non-Asians. It is well known among investigators that they launder their illegally obtained profits by investing in legitimate businesses.

8. Asian Credit Unions

Each Asian ethnic group has their own form of 'credit union.' These unions consist mainly of women members with a total number of from ten to twenty people. The unions are organized for definite periods, by frequency of meetings, and require specific amounts of money on hand. Their purpose is to raise money informally thereby bypassing the controls and bookkeeping of banks and lending institutions. It begins with an agreement among the union members that each will bring a specified amount of money with them to each meeting in order to keep the union's cash holding at a certain level.

During the meeting, each of the members places bids for the total cash holding and the highest bidder receives the cash to use for a period of time. The amount of the winner's bid is paid into the union in the form of interest on the loaned money. In the time allowed by the union, the cash will be paid back and the loan will be available to yet another bidder.

On the surface, Asian credit unions look very good and appear to be nothing more than self-help programs. But they are, by the way they are organized, informal arrangements, with no official safeguards, and always involve large amounts of cash. The informal credit unions have great potential for creating serious problems. On occasion, an organizer of a union will turn out to be untrustworthy and will rig a bidding or abscond with the union's total cash amount. When this happens, the other union members can never fall back on the police for help since the business of the union is illegal in the first place. Union members must either suffer the loss in silence or call on the services of a strong arm element which will attempt to make collection and enforce discipline at the same time.

Many Asians praise these informal programs as 'self help' and 'head start' examples of ethnic togetherness and ingenuity. However, many of these same people who extol the virtues of the 'unions' are quick to point out they have great potential for danger and that many of their fellow countrymen have been victimized by unscrupulous organizers.

Asian credit unions are known by several names. The following list describes them according to the various ethnic groups.(10)

0	Hui	(Vietnamese)
0	Gae	(Korean)
0	Cho Wui	(Chinese)
0	Tana-moshi	(Japanese)

The spelling of the name used by each group's 'union' was arrived at after reading a variety of spellings by several members of each ethnic group. Caution should be exercised regarding the accuracy of these four rough interpretations.

9. Summary

The topics of discussion in this chapter demonstrate that some immigrants from Asia are very knowledgable about ways in which to beat the government system and to exploit their own people. These types of criminal activity are not only harmful to the Asian and non-Asian community, as a whole, but are extremely poor examples of citizenship for their young to emulate as they mature into adults.

The capability to successfully carry out the various schemes such as the importation and distribution of controlled substances, the insurance frauds, currency transfers, asset hiding, the kickbacks, and the 'credit unions' all show a degree of sophistication, organization, and profitability which should alarm all in law enforcement. Asian criminals are often free to pursue whatever course they wish as long as they conduct it inside the Asian community. There, they can operate in an open and uninhibited fashion, without much fear of intervention by law enforcement, and where informant information is seldom understood or acted upon by authorities. The communities in which the criminals presently operate can be assured the course they will take will be an expanding one. Non-Asian communities can expect the expansion to one day impact their lifestyles, as well.

Notes   (1) Virginia Department of Health Regulatory Boards Enforcement Division, Falls Church and Arlington County Police Departments.

(2) U.S. Customs and the Drug Enforcement Administration.

(3) Arlington County Police Department, Virginia.

(4) <u>Author</u>: Although I know of no cases which have been investigated by insurance companies, trusted and reliable sources have shown me bills submitted by their doctors to their insurance companies reflecting services never rendered. Sources say, also, that fees are often split between doctor and patient. Sources state, also, that many other schemes exist involving thefts from insurance companies.

(5) <u>Author</u>: I have one source who was so upset that he wrote to elected officials including the Governor, a U.S. Senator, and his Congressman. Some of his replies were ludicrous and insensitive. The complainer also went to a well-known investigative reporter to no avail. His Congressman's reply is shown in Exhibit 4.

(6) A copy of these hearings can be obtained from the U.S. Government Printing Office. Included are in-depth explanations and testimony of investigators and cooperating Vietnamese.

Notes   (7)   Informant sources from within the local Vietnamese communities allege these activities are common practice throughout the United States.

(8)   <u>Author</u>: These schemes were explained to me by both real estate agents and other knowledgable Asian citizens.

(9)   <u>Author</u>: The hiding of assets is one good reason given to me for the disparity in reporting or the underreporting of crime by Asian victims.

(10) <u>Author</u>: When I mentioned these enterprises by their specific ethnic names each of my Asian contacts was surprised of my awareness in such matters. Several then elaborated upon how a few of the 'lending programs' had collapsed because of unscrupulous organizers.

CHAPTER FIVE

This chapter contains five case summaries with each one representative of a different Asian ethnic group. These selected cases will demonstrate interaction among the different ethnic groups of Asian origin as well as sophistication, scope, complexity, and cultural factors.

1. Japanese Yakuza and U.S. Organized Crime

In September, 1985, a year long investigation conducted by the Drug Enforcement Administration and the Federal Organized Crime Strike Force, arising from an extensive undercover operation into activities of the Japanese Yakuza, concluded with the arrest of three individuals of that organization. The investigation involved the total distribution of 32 pounds of methamphetamine and heroin to undercover agents in Honolulu by the Yakuza. In addition, five persons were arrested in Hong Kong as they prepared to fly to Honolulu while in possession of 4 kilograms of heroin and 10 kilograms of methamphetamines. Earlier in the year, one Yakuza suspect was arrested at the Honolulu International Airport while carrying 6 kilograms of methamphetamines he had brought in from the Far East. A conspiracy to commit murder for hire was also developed against Yakuza members who attempted to hire two persons they believed to be American organized crime figures to murder a member of a rival Yakuza gang. They also asked the organized crime figures to help them smuggle 100 handguns, five machineguns, and the rocket launchers into Japan.

The two would-be organized crime figures were federal agents in disguise. The investigation was international in scope, involving criminal activities in Hawaii,

Japan, Hong Kong, and Taiwan. The investigation grew into a joint effort when it involved the Drug Enforcement Administration; U.S. Customs Service; Federal Bureau of Investigation; U.S. Immigration and Naturalization Service; U.S. Army Criminal Investigations Division; Honolulu Police Department; Alcohol, Tobacco, and Firearms Agency; and the Royal Hong Kong Police.(1)

2. Chinese and Other Ethnic Groups

On September 16, 1985, ten members of the 'United Bamboo' Chinese gang were arrested simultaneously in New York, Houston, and Los Angeles. The ten were charged with narcotics violations, conspiracy to import more than 600 pounds of heroin, possession of 150 pounds of marijuana, attempted extortion, solicitation for a contract murder, conspiracy to distribute marijuana, and racketeering. Although the organization is composed primarily of Chinese and is headquartered in Taiwan, it does not limit its membership to Chinese or its criminal activities to Taiwan. The 'United Bamboo' often inducts new members into its ranks from other Asian ethnic groups such as Thais and Vietnamese. Formed nearly 30 years ago in Taiwan, it now has splinter groups operating outside Taiwan, and for more than six years has had chapters on both coasts of the United States. No one knows, at this time, how big or how many more splinter groups exist. What is known is that the 'United Bamboo' is a force in the criminal world that has in no way been stopped or seriously deterred.

This case was initiated in April 1985 by the New York City Police Department Intelligence Division (See Exhibits 1 and 2). The resulting investigation was conducted jointly by the Federal Bureau of Investigation and the New York City Police Department. Investigative support was also provided from many sources but especially from the states of Texas and California.(2)

This case exemplifies the amount of cooperation among different ethnic groups and the international scope of their activities. It also demonstrates the

'United Bamboo's' sophistication of organization and planning and further demonstrates their willingness to do whatever is necessary to achieve their objectives. Law enforcement officials describe the 'United Bamboo' organization as a world wide criminal enterprise.

Exhibit 1 shows a few of the weapons and ammunition recovered. Exhibit 2 shows a few of the drugs picked up by investigators. Exhibit 3 is the artist's rendering of the United Bamboo's initiation

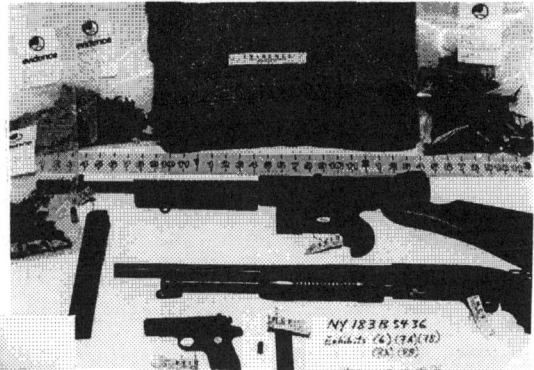

Exhibit 1 - Confiscated Weapons

Exhibit 2 - Confiscated Drugs

rites. In the drawing, jurors see blood-oath video tape taken by undercover officers during a United Bamboo ceremony. The drawing was displayed in the New York Daily News and was part of an article by writer Patrice O'Shaughnessy published August 5, 1986.

Exhibit 3 - The Blood Oath

3. Vietnamese and Non-Asians

As the result of complaints from several Vietnamese citizens living in California, one of the biggest investigations into multimillion dollar fraud in the United States was begun and successfully completed. The complaints were given to the California Attorney General's Medi-Cal Fraud Bureau in March, 1983, and the Bureau was told to investigate possible widespread fraud in the five geographic areas in California where the bulk of the refugees from Southeast Asia reside. Bureau investigators knew the abuse of the Medi-Cal system was large and when they had studied it closely they figured the real losses were actually in excess of 25 million dollars each year during the mid-1980s. Less than a year later, on February 15, 1984, the California Attorney General John K. Van de Kamp, announced the filing of complaints and the issuance of arrest warrants against 34 California physicians, pharmacists, accupuncturists and physicians' assistants on felony charges of Medi-Cal fraud. Felony complaints and arrest warrants were also issued for 17 non-Asians who had assisted in the alleged frauds. The felonies charged included filing false Medi-Cal claims, grand theft, conspiracy, and paying kickbacks.

During the investigation more than thirty search warrants were issued for medical and pharmacy records. Fortunately for the conduct of the investigation, several local police departments in California had developed dependable Vietnamese operatives who were able and willing to interpret books and writings and to go into the businesses to collect what was on public display. The California effort was staffed with ten investigators from the Medi-Cal Fraud Bureau and three investigators from the State Department of Health Services. In addition, the Task Force was assisted by investigators from the California police departments of Westminster, San Jose, San Gabriel, Monterey Park, Pomona, Santa Ana, Garden Grove, Los Angeles and San Diego.(3)

One newspaper headlined the investigation as a crackdown netting 51 Vietnamese. The paper stated some of the profits from the Medi-Cal fraud went directly into drugs which were then diverted to Vietnam's blackmarket.4 It also stated that California has the highest concentration of Indochinese refugees in the nation with more than 240,000 known to authorities with the vast majority of them living in the southern half of the state.

This case demonstrates that sophisticated and well orchestrated fraud schemes can be exposed and prosecuted. It does take, however, great amounts of resources, the full cooperation of local, state, and federal agencies, plus the help of concerned citizens from within the ethnic group.

4. Vietnamese vs Vietnamese

In January 1984 seven young Vietnamese were playing pool together in a pool room frequented only by Asians. Several other Vietnamese lounged about the room or played games nearby. For all purposes, the pool room was just a quiet place where the young Vietnamese spent their time. Suddenly, the quiet was broken as an unknown Vietnamese male entered the room, drew a handgun from a hip pocket, and began shooting at one of the pool players. The target of his shooting was severely wounded by five bullets.

The shooter then fled the room as did a number of the room's occupants. The police were called and when they arrived they found that the victim of the shooting and his six associates were still in the room. The victim of the shooting was quickly removed and taken to the hospital and his six associates were separated and interrogated by investigators. With the aid of a Vietnamese interpreter, the police were able to acquire statements from all six witnesses. Even though the victim and the suspects had been separated before interrogation began, their individual stories were inconsistent, and nothing came of the talks that would help officers with their investigation. It was determined, however, that four of the six witnesses had come from out of town while the remaining two were locals.(5) Each of the remaining six Vietnamese were photographed and fingerprinted. The pictures, prints, and a summary of the shooting, were mailed to police in Houston, Texas, and New Orleans, Louisiana; places where the witnesses said they had residences. Houston police quickly replied that they had been looking for several of the Vietnamese in that city for a series of armed robberies.

New Orleans police did not have any cases pending on any of the Vietnamese witnesses. When the victim was able to converse with police, he quickly picked out his assailant from a group of photographs of Vietnamese the victim had known in New Orleans in past years. The victim told of how he had been involved with his attacker's brother and that the attacker's brother had been harmed at the time. The victim assumed the attacker had heard that several members of the group who had harmed his brother were then in the pool room and had shot at the one that made the easiest and surest target. In time honored fashion, the would-be killer had made his way to the poolroom where he began a shooting that had been on his mind for more than two years. He lived out the Vietnamese adage, "A Vietnamese will nurture a hurt in his heart until the time is ripe for revenge."

This particular Vietnamese case demonstrates several things for the reader. First that the Vietnamese are highly mobile. Second, they are armed and dangerous. And third, they will travel any distance, wait any length of time, and do anything to satisfy a revenge.

5. The Korean 'Mob'

In March 1986, two confidential Korean informants came forward with information concerning extortion, kidnapping, attempted murder, and other criminal activities involving Korean criminals in the Asian community. They claimed the gang specialized in extorting from fellow Koreans. In April, an alleged former ring leader of the 'mob' also came to the police after he had been kidnapped and beaten by other gang members. He was threatened further because the 'mob' had found out he had been operating a gambling casino in Manhattan without the gang's permission.

Local law enforcement agencies and the Federal Bureau of Investigation formed the Joint Organized Crime Task Force and immediately began focussing their resources on the Korean 'Mob.' Soon, undercover officers began advertising themselves as potential gamblers and operators of illegal casinos in both Queens and Manhattan. When 'Mob' members approached the disquised officers and offered them their protection, the Task Force undercover team readily agreed and began making documented payments to the 'Mob' in monthly amounts of from $500 to $1,000.

The Koreans were receptive to the idea and even allowed the investigators some access to their own criminal organization. What the investigators soon found was a major Korean ring which was shaking down more than 40 Korean owned bars and restaurants for hundreds of dollars of protection money each month. They also determined the gang was selling their victims house plants and herbal medicines to cover the received extortion money. The plants and medicines were sold at highly inflated prices.

After six months of undercover investigation, the investigators decided they had all the evidence they needed to make arrests and begin prosecutions of twelve suspects. By this time, also, they had seized the gang's records from which they determined their collections had netted them nearly one million dollars. The seized books also told them the gang had from thirty to forty associate members.

This Korean case, as do the previous stated cases, demonstrates the need for proactive investigations with joint jurisdictional cooperative efforts. It also shows the criminals do expand their base of operations to other cities containing large or significant numbers of their own ethnic groups. The case also reveals that the factors of fear and reprisal continue to be a great hindrance to the prosecution.

6. Summary

These cases, representing each major Asian ethnic group, have several significant factors in common. They all required undercover operatives along with information from concerned citizens. Working the cases also required close inter-agency and inter-jurisdictional cooperation. The sharing of information learned in one case is often beneficial to other jurisdictions as evidenced by the identification of criminal suspects by officials in Houston, Texas on information learned from Arlington, Virginia. Sharing of information and cooperation also goes beyond our national borders. Police must be able to allocate personnel and money for long term investigations, involving these Asian criminal enterprises, because they are nearly always complex and are frequently linked to one another throughout the United States and often to criminal groups in other nations, as well.

Notes (1) This information was accumulated entirely from news media releases since the Strike Force Prosecutor did not return the author's requests for information. This topic is discussed in greater depth in Chapter VII.

(2) Information and pictures provided by the New York City based Task Force comprised of New York City Police and the Federal Bureau of Investigation.

(3) Information provided by Donald Saviers, Chief of Police, Westminster, California.

(4) Santa Ana Register, February 15, 1984, p. A7.

(5) Four were from New Orleans, Louisiana and two from Houston, Texas.

CHAPTER SIX

Law enforcement's response to Asian criminal activity has been a varied approach using traditional programs along with some innovative ones designed during the last decade. In this chapter, we will look at several law enforcement agencies which have dedicated portions of their departments to protective and investigative services for their Asian populations. It is not intended here to critique these agencies or those who have yet to implement these kinds of services.

The primary goal of Chapter Six is to demonstrate that many communities have recognized that Asian crime is growing and have taken steps to counter the problem.

1. New York City, New York

The Intelligence Division of the Police Department has a "desk" assigned to Asian Organized Crime. Several staff members, including an analyst, are assigned to this detail. It is their responsibility to gather information, analyze it, identify trend developments, develop projects on criminal activity and, when appropriate, develop proactive cases.(1)

In the Borough of Manhattan, which contains one of the largest Chinatowns in the United States, there is a special unit under the control of the Borough Commander. This unit is officially known as the Detective Bureau, Manhattan South Task Force 2. It consists of one Oriental Gang Unit. Unofficially, it is known as the 'Jade Squad' and is made up of a sergeant and four detectives. It is their responsibility to monitor the Asian gang activity, assist other units, develop informants and information and, generally, operate as a field unit and make arrests.(2)

The 5th Precinct is headquartered in Chinatown. This Precinct has 150 police officers of which 14 are Asians who speak a Chinese dialect. There are approximately 25 plainclothes officers. Two of the Asian officers are assigned to work the gangs. Both officers are involved in criminal intelligence gathering and law enforcement. One of the pair speaks Chinese.

The below information pertains to the personnel in the 'Jade Squad' and intelligence.

0	Personnel Commitment	- Seven, including one analyst
0	Number of Asian speaking Staff	- Four
0	Approach	- Pro and reactive
0	Size of Asian Population	- 610,000(3)

2. San Francisco, California

Under the umbrella of intelligence gathering and prosecution is the San Francisco Police Department's Gang Task Force(GTF). The GTF was formed in 1976 in response to a multiple homicide in the city's Chinatown. Due to changes in the crime activities of the City, the responsibilities of the GTF has been expanded to cover all gangs regardless of ethnic identification.

The GTF consists of six inspectors who are assigned gang related cases and eight patrolmen who work in plain clothes and in unmarked cars during evening hours throughout the 49 square miles of San Francisco. Cases are assigned to the GTF when there is some evidence of gang relationship. Gang-related homicides are normally passed on to the Department's Homicide Unit for investigation.

0	Personnel Commitment	- Fourteen
0	Number of Asian speaking Staff	- Three
0	Approach	- Pro and reactive
0	Size of Asian Population	- 120,000(4)

3. Arlington County Police, Virginia

Arlington has one officer, a plain clothes detective, whose primary assignment is Asian Criminal Intelligence. His main efforts and the majority of his time is spent in Arlington's Vietnamese community which contains the commercial center for the whole Washington, D.C. metropolitan area's Vietnamese population.(5) This is accomplished by utilizing the old foot beat concept of policing. He gathers criminal information and acts as a liaison between the Vietnamese community, the police department, and other county government agencies.

There is also specific training designed for the local officers. At the recruit level there is instruction in Asian culture. There is a roll call training for patrol officers. It is developed in such a manner as to present the officers with the picture of how things are developing and proceeding within their patrol areas.(6)

The first formalized training in the State of Virginia in Asian crime and Asian community needs occurred in 1987. In July of that year the Northern Virginia Criminal Justice Academy, one of seven regional police academies in the state, presented a four day Asian Crime Seminar in close cooperation with the police departments of Arlington County and New York City. Attendees for this first training effort in law enforcement awareness came from many agencies in the East.

0	Personnel Commitment	- One

0	Number of Asian speaking Staff	- None
0	Approach	- Pro and reactive
0	Size of Asian Population	- 8,000(7)

4. Dallas, Texas

This city has approximately 35,000 Southeast Asian refugees. To address their needs, the department created a storefront operation which is officially called "East Dallas Community - Police and Refugee Liaison Office." It is staffed by sworn police officers, Southeast Asian Public Service Officers, and caseworkers form the Mutual Assistance Associations who assist in the storefront's job referral system.

From this storefront, numerous activities and programs are provided for the community residents. The storefront is active in youth activities, providing food and clothing assistance, presenting crime prevention programs, employment assistance, adult education in the English language, and officer foot patrol of the surrounding neighborhood.(8)

0	Personnel Commitment	- Four
0	Number of Asian speaking Staff	- Three
0	Approach	- General Police/Social services
0	Size of Asian Population	- 35,000

5. Toronto, Canada

Three separate Canadian organizations have combined their manpower and resources to face the Asian crime problem through a Joint Forces Operation approach. Located in Toronto, Ontario, the ten year old Asian Organized Crime Squad consists of eight full-time members from the Toronto Police Department, the Ontario Provincial Police, and the Royal Canadian Mounted Police. Their sole mission is the gathering of Asian crime intelligence.

Part of the Asian Organized Crime Squad is the Asian Crime Unit which serves to provide the general function with an enforcement arm. Composed of both full and part time personnel, the Asian Crime Unit operates with a strength of five patrol officers for community relations purposes and ten plainclothes personnel for investigations and arrests.

0	Personnel Commitment	- Eighteen (plus five part time)
0	Number of Asian speaking Staff	- Four
0	Approach	- Pro and reactive
0	Size of Asian Population	- 330,000

6. Vancouver, Canada

The Joint Task Force was formed by the Vancouver Police and the Royal Canadian Mounted Police to address the area's Asian crime problem. The Operation is divided into two functions:

0   Asian Crime Section staffed with 12 plainclothes officers with the combined responsibiliity of criminal intelligence gathering and law enforcement.

0   Coordinated Law Enforcement Unit consisting of four target teams of 12 to 16 officers each. Conspiracy oriented, the Unit targets organized crime organizations and conducts covert operations in multi-jurisdictions.

0	Personnel Commitment	- Twenty-four to twenty-eight
0	Number of Asian speaking Staff	- One
0	Approach	- Pro and reactive
0	Size of Asian Population	- 150,000

7. Garden Grove, California

Garden Grove is a city of approximately 131,000 citizens and occupies an area of 17 square miles. Initially, the Police Department assigned one man in plainclothes to work in the Vietnamese community. His assignment was to make contacts, develop information, and establish liaison with the community. That has now been expanded considerably. Recently, the Department initiated a storefront operation in their Vietnamese area and plans a second one in their Korean community.

0	Personnel Commitment	- Seven
0	Number of Asian speaking Staff	- Two
0	Approach	- Pro and reactive
0	Size of Asian Population	- 20,000

8. Westminster, California

This department is one of several within Orange County, California and has over 80,000 Vietnamese refugees. Within Westminster is an area which contains the Southeast Asian Cultural Center and the largest Vietnamese business community outside of Ho Chi Minh City.(9)

In a recently completed Asian Center, which will contain several dozen Vietnamese businesses, there will be a storefront operation manned and operated by the Westminster Police Department seven days a week, 10-12 hours per day. Storefront operation hours will be flexible according to what the working staff deem appropriate for the clientele they are attempting to attract. The storefront, donated to the effort by a local business person, consists of 640 square feet of floor space in two offices and a reception area. Its phone lines will be connected directly to the Department and to a police radio monitor. The Westminster store front operation

Exhibit 1 - Westminster Asian Center

Exhibit 2 - Asian Center Artifacts

Exhibit 3 - Westminster Police Office Inside Asian Center

will be staffed by a sergeant and four officers.

0	Personnel Commitment	- Five
0	Number of Asian speaking Staff	- One studying Vietnamese
0	Approach	- Traditional police services
0	Size of Asian Population	- 80,000

9. Philadelphia, Pennsylvania

This city has a very large Asian population. It is primarily made up of Chinese, Koreans, and Vietnamese. The Philadelphia Police Department has an Intelligence Division which has both an Organized Crime Unit and an Intelligence Unit. Both Units have one staff member each assigned to Asian crime problems.

The Organized Crime Unit is an operational and enforcement function while the Intelligence operation remains proactive in what it does. The officer assigned to do intelligence spends much of the working day inside the Asian community and is well known by the Asians that live and work there. The officer's role is to gather information, develop informants, and maintain the police presence.(10)

0	Personnel Commitment	- Two
0	Number of Asian speaking Staff	- None
0	Approach	- Investigative and Enforcement
0	Size of Asian Population	- 80 to 100,000

10. California Department of Justice, Sacramento, California

Within this major department is the Bureau of Organized Crime and Criminal Intelligence which has the responsibility for developing proactive criminal intelligence on a variety of criminal activities. One of its major concerns is Asian gangs in California.

The Bureau, also known as BOCCI, assists those communities experiencing Asian gang problems by providing them with analyses, trends and forecasts, charting, special equipment, central files, and several training programs. They also have a number of Special Agents in the field with each trained to provide on-site guidance and other assistance. The Bureau also produces several yearly reports partially devoted to the Asian crime problem; one for the California State Legislature and another for local agency use.

Also available is the Special Prosecutions Unit composed of special agents and attorneys whose task it is to take cases that might be difficult or impossible to handle at the local level. Some of their cases relate to Asian crime in California. Supporting local agency Asian-related requests, also, is the Department's Bureau of Narcotic Enforcement, the Bureau of Forensic Sciences, and the Bureau of Criminal Information.

0	Personnel Commitment (BOCCI)	- One Analyst
0	Number of Asian speaking Staff	- None
0	Approach	- Proactive
0	Size of Asian Population	- 300 to 350,000

11. Boston, Massachusetts

The Boston Police Department has 1,700 sworn and civilian personnel and an intelligence function consisting of one sergeant and three detectives. One of the assigned detectives is responsible for all of the city's Asian crime problems. In addition to their intelligence duties, the intelligence function is tasked with dignitary protection. To deal with the increasing criminal activity in the Vietnamese business area of Boston, the Department adopted a program developed and used by their

Community Disorders Unit (CDU). The program calls for the establishment of a permanently staffed phone hot line to receive calls from all persons and at all hours of the day and night. When called, the Department dispatches field units which the Department has positioned at strategic points in the city. At this writing, the CDU approach has been partially successful in its results and overwhelmed by the additional duties the 'approach' has required. Recently, the Boston Police Department has begun assigning a team of three or four of its personnel to investigate Asian crimes on a case by case basis.

0	Personnel Commitment	- One
0	Number of Asian speaking Staff	- None
0	Approach	- Reactive and information
0	Size of Asian Population	- 40,000

12. Portland, Oregon

This city is unique in that the Portland School District has its own police which are commissioned law enforcement officers. Local authorities report school police are very effective in preventing criminal activities from developing among school age Asian youth.

The City of Portland Police Department has no designated special function or emphasis upon Asian crime. They do, however, have several 3rd generation Chinese and Japanese officers in the Department.

0	Personnel Commitment	- None
0	Number of Asian speaking Staff	- None
0	Approach	- No specific program
0	Size of Asian Population	- 20,000(11)

13. Seattle, Washington

In 1983, there was an Asian mass murder in Seattle which encouraged the Seattle Police Department to create an Asian Investigative Squad. Over the years and as major crimes diminished in the Asian community, the original focus upon the Asian crime problem changed. As other ethnic gangs surfaced and began to create the majority of the city's crime problems, the Police Department expanded its commitment and broadened its investigative interests. Seattle now has a Coordinated Crime Investigations Unit of six persons responsible for all gang related activities and investigations. One officer in their intelligence operation has the responsibility for Asian Organized Crime and ethnic gang drug activity.

0	Personnel Commitment	- Seven (General duties)
0	Number of Asian speaking Staff	- One
0	Approach	- Pro and reactive
0	Size of Asian Population	- 50,000

14. New Jersey State Police

The New Jersey State Police is a very active and progressive agency. It has a force of 2,200 sworn officers of which 21 are Asians. Their Intelligence Services Section (ISS) consists of 75 sworn persons and 15 civilian analysts. The ISS is divided into two groups; traditonal and non-traditional organized crime.

Non-traditional organized crime includes Asian and Jamacian crimes and motorcycle gangs. The Asian portion of the function is comprised of three Asian specialists.

0	Personnel Commitment	- Three

0   Number of Asian speaking Staff   - None (Asian Troopers)
0   Approach   - Proactive
0   Size of Asian Population   - 60,000

15. Australia

According to the Australian Bureau of Statistics, the current population of Australia is nearly sixteen million of which 341,000 are of Asian origin. A further breakdown shows that nearly a fourth of the Asians are Vietnamese (92,687). The largest concentrations of Vietnamese are found in the states of Victoria and New South Wales.

0   Victoria

In 1985, the Victoria Police initiated a special investigation group called the *Bao Ve Investigation Group*,(12) whose primary objective was the investigation of extortion within the Vietnamese community in the city of Melbourne. The Police Department organized and conducted a Vietnamese language and culture course for its officers and initiated several other programs as well to support their desire to improve police services and deter crime in the Asian community. Two of the programs included a 24 hour hotline for Vietnamese use and a Police/Ethnic Affairs Annual Award for members of the Police Force who have most contributed to the building of improved relations between Victoria Police and the ethnic communities. The persons receiving the awards are selected by leaders of the various Asian communities.

0   Personnel Commitment   - Six
0   Number of Asian speaking staff   - One
0   Approach   - Pro and reactive
0   Size of Asian Population   - 85,000

0   New South Wales

The New South Wales Police have identified crimes in the Asian communities and have undertaken several long range strategies to bring them under control. Their approach now includes increased foot patrols in the areas where crimes are being committed, the use of multi-lingual business cards, telephone call-in services, training in Asian language and culture, and individual officers speaking before Asian community groups.

0	Personnel Commitment	- None
0	Number of Asian speaking Staff	- None
0	Approach	- Reactive (Developing Strategy)
0	Size of Asian Population	- 30,000+

0   South Australia

The Police Department reported that their crime incidents involving Asians are not significant. Their multi-cultural Services Staff have daily contact with the Asian communities with particular emphasis on the Vietnamese citizens. The Staff works closely with the operational police whenever there is the possibility of crimes occurring or impacting the Asian community.

The Police Department sponsors regular educational programs during which the role of law enforcement is described and other topics are covered. Much of this information is made available to the Asian community through local newsletters. Members of the Police Department also meet periodically with Asian business persons when there are matters involving crime or potential crime.

0	Personnel Commitment	- Five
0	Number of Asian speaking Staff	- None

| 0 | Approach | - Liaison and Resource |
| 0 | Size of Asian Population | - 16,000+ |

0   <u>Tasmania</u>

The first Vietnamese settled in Tasmania in 1980 where they received orientation and introduction into Australian life and the new standards of living. Tasmanian Government support programs continued for several years and were phased out in 1986. By 1988, many Vietnamese families elected to move elsewhere in Australia leaving only several hundred of their number in Tasmania.

Tasmanian Police report that they have never had any significant crime problems involving their Asian citizens.

0	Personnel Commitment	- None
0	Number of Asian Speaking Staff	- None
0	Approach	- None
0	Size of Asian Population	- 2,300+

16. Three Initiatives

Three practices that seem to be highly effective in bridging the cultural/ethnic gaps between the Asian community and the local police are:

0   Law enforcement advertisements or notifications in the Asian media
0   Using law enforcement business cards which have been printed in the Asian languages
0   Maintaining a law enforcement phone 'hot line' dedicated totally to calls from the Asian community

These three initiatives above were designed and tested in Arlington, Virginia in order to maximize exposure of local police services and to make the services more easily available and understandable to the Asian community.

The calling cards were designed in such a fashion as to show the Asians police awareness of their languages, the dragon in their cultures, and the obvious closeness between the various ethnic groups, i.e., Chinese and Vietnamese. The newspaper articles are in the form of an open letter to the community as a whole. These letters dealt with issues which were of major concern to the Vietnamese community at the time of their release.

These initiatives are not solutions in themselves. They are simply several attempts to catch the interest of the Asian community and to show them that government is not only acutely aware of their crime problems but willing to do something about them.

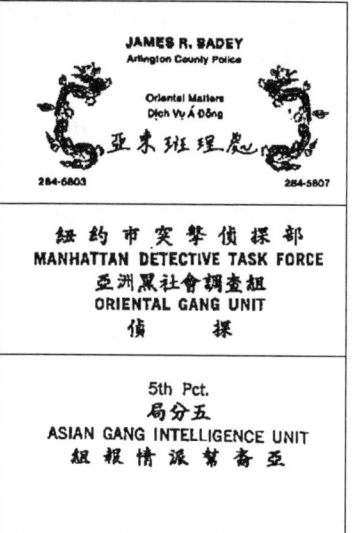

Exhibit 2 - Three Cards

The publisher has composed a series of investigative and information forms in the written languages of several Asian groups that can, when used correctly, bridge the difficult language barrier between Asian refugees and law enforcement. There is one form for each of the following ethnic groups: Chinese; Vietnamese; and Japanese. Users of these forms must keep in mind that they were designed for the sole purpose of acquiring 'first contact' information only and not intended to be used as final collection documents. These forms were designed to 'break the ice,' so-to-speak, thus avoiding the lack of understanding posture that so often follows questioning when interpreters are not readily available.

17. Warnings

Several warnings regarding the use of these forms are in order. Some Asians are illiterate in their own languages and may suffer a 'loss of face' when asked to read a form they are expected to understand. Therefore, use of the information collection forms must be conditioned on the officer's knowledge of the literacy of the Asian contributor.

Included also in the forms package are Miranda Warnings written in each of the three languages. It is important to remember that any use of these Miranda forms without the <u>direct help of competent interpreters</u> can later cause problems in court. The emphasis remains on whether the contributor understands his or her rights and, with these rights in mind, gives the information willingly. Should there be any doubt regarding this understanding, the court will most likely declare the use of a Miranda Warning null and void.

Permission is hereby given to law enforcement agencies by the Publisher to use the three collection forms and the Miranda Warnings displayed in Appendix A-1.

18. Summary

The departments contributing to this book are just a sampling of different approaches taken by police administrators in confronting Asian crime problems. There are many other departments with similar programs but to list them all would be nothing more than repetition. On the other hand, there are many local departments whose communities contain significant Asian populations and who have chosen either to ignore the growing crime problems or are attempting to deal with them with their existing police programs and resources.

There is a consistent theme in recommendations produced by this limited survey. Whether the recommendations come from Australia, Canada, California, Texas, New York or Virginia, they always contain elements of the following:

0   Liaison must be established with the Asian community

0   Avenues for the transfer of information from the Asian community to the police department must be in place

0   Special education and training in Asian needs and culture must be provided to all members of the department

No one person can say which program is the best or the correct program. It is the responsibility of each police administrator to determine the needs of their local community and then provide the means for the department to best serve those needs. Whatever course of action is implemented, it must be done with the ability to be flexible and with the courage to be innovative.

19. Chapter Contributors

Special thanks to the following persons who contributed information on their departments and operations for Chapter Six. They include: Sergeants Bobby Lum and James McVeety, New York Police Department; Sergeant Dan Foley and Bill Murphy, San Francisco Police Department; Corporal Ron Cowart, Dallas Police Department; Sergeants George Cowley and Ken Yates, Toronto Police Department; and Constable A. Turner, Vancouver, Canada Police Department, Chief of Police Donald Saviers, Westminster Police Department; Sergeant Joe Rudy, Philadelphia Police Department; Administrator of Intelligence Jack Morris, California Department of Justice; Detective Mike Keller, Houston Police Department; Detective Gary Fowler, Seattle Police Department; Detective Kathy Johnston, Boston Police Department; Detective Gary Fantz, Portland Police Department; Detective Sergeant Charles Smith, New Jersey State Police; Lieutenant David Abrecht, Garden Grove Police Department, California; Detective Senior Constable Kevin

Curran, Victoria, Australia; Chief Superintendent O.L.W. Bevan, South Australia; Divisional Detective Inspector A.R. Anstey, Tasmania, Australia; and Chief Inspector Rex Anderson, New South Wales.

Notes   (1) Dignitary protection is relegated to the Intelligence Division and this responsibility takes precedence over their primary assigned duties. Intelligence and dignitary protection are each full time tasks. To place both these responsibilities in one unit is a great burden on the individuals and one or the other of the two tasks suffers, as a result.

(2) The 'Jade Squad' was formed in the mid-1970's in response to a multiple homicide in Chinatown.

(3) The Borough of Manhattan alone has 300,000 in its Chinatown.

(4) The figure, 120,000 Asians, represents slightly more than 21 percent of the city's total population.

(5) This commercial center is in the process of change stimulated by community area improvements. It is anticipated that this Asian community will undergo massive change. Many, if not all, of the present Asian home owners and businesses may be forced to relocate a short distance away in neighboring Falls Church, Virginia.

(6) Every police recruit going through the Northern Virginia Criminal Justice Academy receives a two hour block of instruction in Asian culture. This training is an awareness program. It emphasizes the difference between Asian and American cultures. The roll call training is presented

Notes   on a timely basis either upon request by supervisors or as conditions change and situations occur in the Vietnamese community.

(7) This figure is from 1987 and represents a quadrupling of their number since the 1980 census. In addition to the Southeast Asians, there are about 3,000 Chinese, Japanese, and Koreans according to the 1980 census.

(8) Corporal Ron Cowart of the Dallas Police Department was the main force in organizing and implementing this storefront operation. He saw a special need and, with determination, set about to make things happen. This operation deals with both Asian and Hispanic immigrants.

(9) From a statement made by Donald Saviers and then given to the President's Commission on Organized Crime, October 17, 1984.

(10) These officers feel that this modification and application of the foot beat concept is paramount in developing contributors and information. The continual presence of police officers is proof of the Department's commitment. The use of plain clothes persons overcomes the stigma of uniformed officers which is commonly found in the minds of Asians.

(11) Southeast Asians, Chinese, Koreans, and Japanese.

(12) The Vietnamese words, *Bao Ve*, literally translated in this context as 'to protect.'

CHAPTER SEVEN

The determination of the need to use an interpretor or translator is evident and, in many cases, unavoidable. However, the selection of the proper interpretor is of paramount importance.

To begin with, the person who is going to be used to listen and translate must, above all, be neutral. The individual must have no vested interest in the outcome of the case. Anything other than total neutrality can result in the interpreter editing what he hears and only passing on to investigators that which aids his personal interest; such as placing his family or ethnic group in a better light than it deserves.

1. The Selection Process

In picking one translator candidate from among several, the selector must always be aware of, and sensitive to, cultural issues. The following examples demonstrate the need for understanding the various cultures.

0   The Social Status of the Translator

A former Asian male military officer who served in Vietnam during the war might very well find it offensive to be questioned by someone whom he knows once was an enlisted man in his organization. On the other hand, the same enlisted man might be extremely uncomfortable talking with the former officer. The communication between the two might be unnecessarily impaired just because the investigators failed to sense the importance of their differing social status.

0   Marital Status and Age Differences

A 42 year old Vietnamese married woman was a rape victim.   Investigators quickly determined that a language barrier existed between them and the woman and that an interpreter was needed. They located a 30 year old single Vietnamese woman and brought the two together. The interview was over before it had begun. Although they spoke the same language, they could not relate and both were extremely embarrassed over the subject being discussed in the interview. The investigators decided to try another interpreter who was married and was several years older than the victim. The two women were able to talk frankly and soon the story was in the hands of the investigators.

0   Motivation of the Interpreter

Another equally important factor is the motivation of the the person doing the interpreting. As an example, one experienced police investigator indicated he had a great Vietnamese translator he used whenever he had a crime to investigate in his 'Little Saigon.' When asked if the translator worked for his police department he replied, "No." He then told a story about how a good looking girl just came in one day and offered her services as a translator of the Vietnamese and Chinese languages. He added, "So I used her."

As with any off the street informant, law enforcement officers should always ponder the motivation for such unsolicited cooperation. Special thought should be given to this form of assistance when it comes from someone in an Asian community - - and more so yet, when it is from someone who is young.

Interpreters become the linchpins in investigations. They soon know more than the investigators and they know who is doing the talking and who is being identified. Before an interpreter is used, investigators should concern themselves with their background, dependability, integrity, their associations, their skills at translating and, most importantly, their reasons for assisting.

It must always be remembered the association of the official interpretor with the police will soon become known throughout the Asian community. Little is known how far beyond the community that word of the relationship will travel but it can be assumed it crosses the continent when it is important enough to be known both near and far. A few obvious reasons why an Asian would come forward and provide translator services without urging include:

0   Community assistance
0   Develop relationship with the police
0   Financial reward
0   Counter-intelligence

Hopefully, the vast majority of Asian contributors come in for the first three reasons; that is to help the community, to develop a closer relationship with the police, and/or to earn some easy money. There is always a small chance, however, one may offer his help because he has been directed to do so by some gang or organization purely for penetrating the investigation or the overall police system.

Investigators are obliged, therefore, to carefully guard against the development of an association between them and their Asian assistants that may be used to manipulate their investigations or to reduce their credibility within Asian communities. This potential for manipulation is not limited to Asians, however, since it is often encountered between law enforcement personnel and their sources regardless of ethnic backgrounds. The basic rules that are described here should provide guidance in this important area.

0   Several Basic Rules

The first rule is that translators should always write the words down exactly as they are given. They should never be allowed to write their interpretation of words in anyway other than the way they are delivered. Interpretation can verbally occur between the investigator and the translator only when additional clarity is needed in the writing of the official police report.

Second, consider translators as nothing more than confidential sources of information who must be trained, controlled, and directed during all periods of their assignments.   A number of rules given by Morris in his book, Police Informant Management, hold true here also.(1)   Morris emphasized the importance of knowing sources, keeping sources apart, corroborating their information, and evaluating their credibility. The translator can be guided into being one of the most productive persons in an investigation by following these canons of source control and use.

2. Interviews and Interrogations

All interviews and interrogations of Asians work best when the investigators are sensitive to cultural issues. When the culture and history of the ethnic group is understood, an investigator can appreciate the Asian's thought process and points of reference. Without this sensitivity, little is gained and much time is lost.

0   Knowing The Small Things

It helps when investigators can reflect on an Asian religious concept or attitude toward something such as their concept of time. For instance, the Vietnamese do not take schedules very seriously. They have an expression reflecting this attitude: "Time is like rubber," meaning life is flexible. When making an appointment with a

Vietnamese, it is always important to specify whether the appointment is on 'American time' or 'Vietnamese time.' The understanding here is with American time you are punctual and precise. With Vietnamese time, you have a lot of leeway and showing up 30 or 40 minutes after the appointed time is completely acceptable. Knowing such small things about their way of life does not demonstrate how clever or smart investigators are but rather simply develops a relationship in the most expedient manner possible.

When scheduling an interview or conducting an interrogation be prepared for a long session. Never be in a hurry. Take plenty of time while you move slowly toward the subject of your visit. Stay professional even when the investigation continues to bog down in pointless or irrelevant discussion. Some shortcuts to getting to the point of your meeting are to avoid police jargon, technical terms, law book quotes, and figures of American speech.

It is highly important to practice the art of sitting in silence without showing that your patience has reached its end. After all, you have come for information and if you are willing to work for it, eventually it will be brought out.

Bluffs fail most of the time since many Southeast Asians are not moved by the threat of possibly going to jail. As an example of their lack of fear for jail is the following true story. A young Vietnamese gang member was serving thirty days in the county jail when he was visited by the detective that had arrested him. The detective told him that he had better behave himself when he went back to the street or he'd end up right back in jail.

"That's O.K.," he said, "when I come to jail, I was sick and they give me medicine. I have three meals a day, not Vietnamese, but still good. I have a bed every night. The jail is air conditioned. I have television. Tomorrow when I get out they give me money." He shrugged his shoulders as if to say how could he have it better.

Within 36 hours, he was arrested again and returned to jail. He bonded out again and this time left the jurisdiction. Several months later he was arrested in another state for killing two men and wounding a third with a shotgun. Jail was of no consequence to him and is one example of why many Asian experts among law enforcement believe jailing holds little fear for Asian criminals overall.

0   Much Preliminary Discussion

When talking with Vietnamese, investigators can expect to discuss many non-investigative subjects before any time is devoted to the business at hand. It should come as no surprise to investigators when they spend their first minutes - - sometimes hours - - talking about the Asian's family, his business, and his background. Investigators should encourage this to some degree, given there is time for such preliminaries, for patience in the beginning will later sow a bountiful harvest of information.

This preliminary discussion is according to Asian custom and, when done right and with sincerity, will allow them to become comfortable in the presence of the police and to begin talking more openly. It is important to get past the threatening opening stages that precede all police investigations. Once the Asians are comfortable with the manner of police business, they very often will show how gracious they can be.

0   Sharing Common Experiences

If possible, the sharing of personal background antidotes with some Asians helps to develop the first opening rapport. A young Vietnamese once told the author how poor his family was in Vietnam. He said that when they ate dinner, each member of the family had a small bowl of rice in front of them. In the middle of the family spread there was a piece of wood carved in the shape of a fish. He said that as they ate their rice they each pointed to the carved wood. In doing so, they felt as though they had actually partaken of the fish.

The author listened and remembered a story that had been told to him about the potato famine in Ireland. He told the Vietnamese that the Irish poor would sit around, much like the Vietnamese, only they had individual potatoes to consume. In the middle of their table was a small piece of meat. As they ate, each member pointed at the meat until the dinner was over.

Sharing stories can help bridge the cultural gap. No story should ever be offered by the investigator that exposes a police strategy, names witnesses or sources, or otherwise provides confidential information. No rapport building is worth breaching confidence or violating the tenets of need-to-know and right-to-know.

3. Informants and Operatives

As pointed out in Chapter Five, case initiation and successful investigation is sometimes directly attributable to good Asian informants and operatives. Since the Asian community is a difficult place to recruit contributors of information and a near impossible place for non-Asians to penetrate, one must ask, where do these informants come from and how can they be developed?

Traditionally, informants and operatives cooperate with police forces in their investigations because of a number of reasons. Primary among the reasons are survival, emotion, reward, nuisance, and chance.(2) Many experienced officers believe the average criminal works with them to either work off potential charges or for cash. While these motivations may be true for the vast majority of criminals, they do not necessarily fit the motives of Vietnamese and other Asian ethnic groups. Many officers working with Asian informants and operatives find them willing to assist for entirely different reasons which do not include 'working off charges' or for cash. Some will say they are 'concerned citizens' when asked why they are assisting. For the most part, they seemed willing because there had developed a personal rapport and relationship in which both the investigators and their Vietnamese contributors accepted familial roles while using the titles of brother, uncle, sister, and the like.

Undoubtedly, there are much deeper seated reasons for their actions. Determining these reasons would require the services of trained psychologists. But just as in dealing with interpretors, law enforcement must maintain their vigilance in determining the motivations of both "volunteer" walk-in informants and operatives and those who have been recruited and cultivated. Always a major concern is whether an operative or informant is making himself available in order to work with both law enforcement and the criminal element.

Southeast Asian operatives and informants take their actions very seriously. Most can be expected to be rather expert at translating both what they hear and what they read. Some show signs of enjoying being involved in a form of spying and the more it compares with what can be described as 'palace intrigue,' the more they respond to the tasks.

They appear very happy and pleased with themselves when they have successfully completed assignments. Never forget, however, that it bothers them when their fellow Vietnamese have been caught or implicated in criminal activities. Often the Vietnamese contributor will be outraged by what he hears or observes and will go to great lengths to assist investigators in countering possible entrapment complaints while still efficiently getting the task of developing information completed.

0   Observable Anxiety

It has been noted that some Vietnamese contributors show obvious anxiety at the close of their assignments. At some point after their work has concluded they often begin to rationalize about the Vietnamese criminals and wonder why it was they committed their crimes. Much of this anxiety can be attributed to their concern for the family members of the criminals who are still living in Vietnam and who rely upon these nefarious activities to keep alive. This concern partially explains why some Vietnamese contributors, driven as they are to serve their communities, will wait long periods of time before returning to assist the police again in translator or informant assignments.

0   Contributor Feedback

When a case is being developed, there is nothing wrong with running the most cursory aspects of it past the Vietnamese contributor as long as nothing is being said or provided that would in any way assist the criminal targets. What is released must be purely public information and not cover the intended strategy of the investigation or other facts and figures which cannot be shared with non-law enforcement persons. The issue here, while taking great care not to say more than is absolutely necessary about the investigation, is to develop voluntary feedback from the contributor. After all, it is the Asian contributor who understands the minds, activities, and languages of the criminals and it is he who is the real expert in the cases.

As in the handling of informants in non-Asian cases, so the rules apply for the Asian contributor. As Morris said in his book on informant management, ". . .the control officer is always in charge. If the control officer cannot dominate the contributor in every action the two perform together, it is surely better that the contributor be immediately discarded regardless of the consequences to the case."(3)

There will be times when the Asian information gatherer, be that person informant, operator, translator, or interpreter, will attempt to assume the lead role in the case at hand. If the lead investigator is not astute enough to catch the first indications of this attempted role change, then he may not sense until well into the investigation that he has been only responding to what his Asian assistant has deemed important and timely enough to report. He has not, for some time, been following the dictates or needs of his own department. The role change may not occur because of any hidden agenda by the Asian assistant or for any nefarious reasons. Its origin may be much more obvious and occurs simply because the investigator lacked leadership and dominance and, too often, demonstrated to his interpreter that he knew too little about the Asian language and culture. In short, the more the investigator displays a reliance on the Asian assistant for what is said and done by the Asian criminals, the more the interpreter shifts from mere aide to unofficial leader.

Leadership in case work seems to be the natural tendency when using Asians on purely Asian crime matters. Control over what the Asian contributor collects, reports, and becomes involved in must always be at the discretion and direction of the investigator. Only the investigator can call 'all the shots.'

When the investigator feels his Asian assistant is beginning to dictate who, why, when, where, and how investigations should be conducted, a tactful private 'sitdown' meeting is definitely in order. Being tactful means treating the relationship between officer and interpreter in the original business-like manner. By remaining tactful, the officer is able to reconvey his directions, set new schedules, and generally reassert himself as the leader without showing concern over the possible role change.

0   Sharing Asian Contributors of Information

Informants, operators, interpreters, and translators will, on occasion, be asked to assist with other departmental investigations and to even do work for other law enforcement agencies. A common rule among these Asian contributors is that they will nearly always stay in close contact with the officer who first recruited and developed them. This they do in order to gain his advice and to seek his approval for what they are doing and sharing their knowledge. This occasional 'checking in' with their original control officer is proof of their continued reliance upon him/her as a person they trust and admire.

It is not atypical for Asian contributors working for other units to call their original controller and advise him of their new task and to discuss details they have have exposed. Even though you may not want such intimate knowledge of the other case, and tell your source so, the Asian contributor is not likely to understand your rationale. To him, you are his true controller whom he is conditioned to report on when and what he knows. Even after being told to stop providing the details of their assistance to other cases, they may still check in with dates and times of future meetings with the control officers of other agencies. Unless stopped, they may add intimate details of their assignments, the results of their past work, and the general progress of the other investigation.(4)

The investigator must always remember that good insider Asians with a willingness to contribute to law enforcement investigations are hard to find. When located, they must be handled with extreme care by investigators all the while remembering that the contributors have placed themselves not only in danger of destroying themselves socially but are now in great physical danger, as well.

4. Corruption

Many Asian business persons are programmed to paying 'taxes' to law enforcement, politicians, and other enforcement agencies. Because of their past dealings with police and governments in Asia, it is hard for them to see that western law enforcement do their personal jobs without 'under the table' payments. It makes no difference if the payments are free meals, cash, or other forms of gratuity. Whatever the gifts, they are payments for doing business by Asian standards. In one Asian community in the United States, several business people quietly offered goods and services to the detective assigned to their community. The detective happened to know the frequent offers of food and clothing were only a form of payment and he consistently rejected them. He always declared his rejections in a friendly but highly public display. Regardless of his rejections, the offers continued to occur each and every time he entered their businesses while on official duty.

In due time, and as experts on Asian culture would have predicted, the offers of gifts increased in their value and now they took on the form of cash out of the sales registers. Behind each of these offerings was always the friendly smiles of the merchants, their wives, and their hired help who might chance by during the attempted transactions. Everything about the gift-giving was warm and friendly and always gave the impression these merchants offered gifts to everyone who entered. Sometimes the merchants mentioned the wives and children of the investigators by stating the gift of a few dollars could assist the officer's family members toward their school books and clothing. The Vietnamese believe everyone has a price and therefore they were just trying to determine the detective's price.

Investigators assigned to Asian communities should be well aware that gifts to officials are the first step in Asian corruption of government.

Initial corruption begins with the friendly merchant refusing to accept money for a consumed cup of tea or cutting a dinner meal in half for the family of an officer. Later, the corruption attempt becomes more obvious with the offering of a Christmas gift of liquor or oriental artifact. Finally, it may be money. Many Asians believe that most government officials, including the police, have their price. They will attempt to determine the price of each government official with whom they must do business by first offering small, inexpensive things and then move to a fistful of dollars or higher amounts dependent upon the level of the person and the need to develop him as a contact. For many Asians, this is thought of as paying 'taxes.' The size of the taxes is determined by increasing the offerings until the targetted official accepts something.

Should an officer be unaware of what is happening, as the result of the Asian gift giving, he will soon realize the Asian businessman has begun to announce around the community he has a 'friend downtown' who will cut through 'red tape' for him or is available to provide him protection.

There is only one way to stay free of such collusion which is to turn down all offers of free gifts each time they are offered.

5. Education and Training

Law enforcement education and training has made tremendous strides in the last 20 years. Today, many departments require at least two years of college and many officers have gone on to acquire four year degrees, Masters, and even Doctorates. Police officers receive firearms training at least twice a year and most will retire without ever having 'fired a shot in anger' or in the 'heat of battle.' Most states in the United States and in other nations, as well, mandate by law that police officers take a certain amount of certified training courses in a variety of job-related subjects. In spite of all this recent advancement in law enforcement training, there remains a great void in classroom exposure to Asian crime.

0   Asian Specialists

A brief survey of Asian specialists in law enforcement agencies shows there are very few required courses in any schools, including police academies, that deal strictly with Asian crime and Asian criminals. Most officers acquire their knowledge of the general subject by trial and error. Many Asians who could be contributors of criminal information have been driven away and beyond the reach of investigators because of many officers who have errored in the process. Many officers do not wish to dig deeply into the subject or long enough to develop an appreciation for the many cultural differences that exist between Asians and non-Asians.(5)(6)

    0   Chief Executive Officers

Law enforcement administrators also lack a general feel for the size and complexities of the Asian crime phenomenon and do not seem to have regular seminars and workshops in which to turn to for Asian crime information. Without the support of informed Chief Executive Officers, departments responsible for policing Asian communities are not likely to use the proper strategy or commit the kinds of resources necessary to counter the Asian crime problem until it is already headline news. Many administrators do not realize that in the middle of their city is an Asian community rife with unreported and unaccounted for crime whose citizens cry out for help. Only a major change in official awareness will provide the correct responses for satisfying that cry.(7)(8)

    0   The Judicial

Judges and other officers of the court know little about Asian crime and even less about the subleties of culture and how it affects everyday life in the Asian community. Yet, it is the judicial that makes the decisions to prosecute, jail, or let walk on the streets 'the poor little refugee' who has been extorting, assaulting, burning businesses, trafficking in drugs and prostitution, evading taxes, and laundering great amounts of money.

6. Summary

It is not just the police personnel and investigators on the street who need the education and training to understand and effectively deal with Asian criminals and victims but every person in the criminal justice system. As long as the justice system continues to exist in the dark on the Asian crime problem, it will allow these criminal enterprises to flourish and broaden the credibility gap between the justice system and the Asian citizens it is supposed to serve. There should be at least three levels of training for law enforcement as is now being done in California and Virginia. One level of training should be devoted entirely to investigators and intelligence officers who are required to deal directly with Asian victims and offenders. Of concern, also, is the training for middle managers such as sergeants, lieutenants, and captains whose strong support is needed in order to guide law enforcement strategy and to provide resources. Finally, the Chief Executive Officers require periodic awareness programs to make them more knowledgeable about the size of the Asian crime problem in their jurisdictions and across the country and what strategies are available for successful Asian crime control and eradication.

Notes   (1) Jack Morris, <u>Police Informant Management</u>, Palmer Enterprises, 1983, pp. III-10-12.

(2) Ibid., Morris, p. II-2.

(3) Ibid., Morris, p. III-8.

(4) <u>Author</u>: I found this very trying and have never found a tactful way of preventing or stopping it. To hang up the phone would be tantamount to a slap in the face of the contributor. I have felt it wise to listen and conclude with a simple word of thanks.

(5)   The California Department of Justice sponsors several programs aimed at developing awareness for law enforcement intelligence officers regarding Asian crime.   One is a two week program, the <u>Criminal Intelligence Institute</u>, which uses a Vietnamese crime situation as the subject of its daily exercise. For information, contact: Chief, Advanced Training Center, California Department of Justice, 4949 Broadway, Sacramento, Ca., 94203.   The Department also hosts an <u>Asian Gang Conference</u> each year. For information contact: Asian Crime Desk, DOJ/ BOCCI, 4949 Broadway, Sacramento, Ca., 94203.

(6) The Northern Virginia Criminal Justice Academy presented a 32 hour <u>Asian Crime Seminar</u> in 1987 and is scheduling a second program for 1988.

Notes   (7) The California Department of Justice hosts a <u>Chief Executive Seminar</u> on the subject of major crime each year for senior law enforcement executives. One important aspect of the three day program is several hours of high level discussions on Asian crime. For information, contact: Chief, Advanced Training Center, 4949 Broadway, Sacramento, Ca., 94203.

(8)   The Chiefs of Police of Northern Virginia recently had a one day training seminar on Asian crime in which the author served as instructor. The seminar was sponsored by the Northern Virginia Criminal Justice Academy.

CHAPTER EIGHT

The number of Asian refugees residing in the United States, Australia, Canada, and elsewhere outside of Southeast Asia has grown rapidly over recent years and will continue to grow. As these numbers increase, it is evident that more and more Asians will become involved in crime; both as victims and as criminals. Law enforcement officers have already discovered that this group of people presents new and, often, puzzling problems which are not easily or quickly handled through more traditional approaches. The cultural differences are many. Stereotyping of different groups of Asians has created a mystique about them which tends to confuse and compound the problems of dealing with them. Many Asians now residing in their new homelands are recent arrivals who have little knowledge of the English language or understanding of the new governmental system. This tends to make crime investigations, interviews, and interrogations difficult, if not impossible.

1. Resettlement

Readers are reminded that Asians are not unique to the typical patterns of immigration. A general historical view of immigration to the United States, for example, reveals that new arrivals continue to gravitate toward large cities and to live in small, readily identifiable areas. Like the immigrants before them they, too, have found it is easier to live in quasi-cultural microcosms than attempt full social, economic integration into the existing cultural milieu of their new homelands. In fact and with few exceptions, it can be argued that, for them as a group, full social and economic integration into the new homelands is impossible.

Historically, as immigrant groups become more mobile and begin to disperse throughout a greater area in the United States, neighborhoods lose a particular ethnic identity or are replaced by new and different groups; however, total assimilation takes a number of generations, if it ever takes place. To this day, Americans still refer to the Pennsylvania Dutch, the Boston Irish, the Cajuns of Louisiana, and many areas in large cities are still considered as Irish, Italian, Jewish, Black, German, Chinese, and so forth. In more recent years 'Little Saigons' have been added to the list of 'Little Italys.' Similar references; i.e., 'Little India,' 'Little Seoul,' are also heard when referring to neighborhoods in cities occupied by other ethnic Asian groups.

2. Assimilation Barriers

While many ethnic groups have been easily integrated into the work force, a large number lack the English language skills prerequisite to attaining higher levels of education and job skills; all of which are basic to the integration process because minimal language skills and lower educational levels tend to isolate and deny opportunity for advancement in society. People who do not speak the language of the country in which they reside tend to stay with their 'own kind' and it is difficult for them to move freely within the society and become aware of all that society may have to offer.

3. Exclusiveness

There are 'newcomers' (the new arrivals), 'old-timers' (members of the same ethnic group who have been in the United States longer or ethnic groups with whom 'newcomers' have had contact in the old country), and the 'outsiders' (everyone else). The 'newcomers' seek out the 'old-timers' and move into their neighborhoods. These groups and the neighborhoods in which they live are exclusive, unless the existing ethnic make-up of the local area or availability of housing in the given area makes it impossible. Nevertheless, what the neighborhood cannot provide is provided by the ethnic group's religious organizations, shops, businesses, and restaurants.

Another factor which contributes to this exclusiveness is the cultural traditions which they bring as part of their baggage. As marketplaces in Asia are traditional social centers, it should not be surprising to find that ethnic shopping centers in the United States provide a multitude of services not found in a United States supermarket. Restaurants provide a place to entertain friends, conduct business and, lastly, a place to eat. Asians tend to conduct business over a meal rather than at the office. Moreover, Asians entertain friends and important guests in restaurants, rarely at home. They try to live a life which is as close to the one they had in their homeland before coming to the United States. This tends to slow down the acculturation process and makes these communities in-bred and not very outgoing. It is this initial exclusiveness which is regarded with a good deal of suspicion on the part of the 'outsiders' because the 'outsiders' do not understand the language, culture, and social mores of the 'newcomers.'

The family is the primary social unit in Asia; people outside of the family unit are not trusted. Friends are developed early in life; through friends of the family, in school, or later in life through introductions by a network of close friends. While Americans have a tendency to treat even the most casual meeting as friendship, this is not the case in Asia. When an Asian refers to a friend, he or she is making reference to the closest relationship they have outside of the family. Friends of friends are facilitators and friends can be relied upon for many favors which would be out of the question in many western communities. This traditional reliance on all members of the extended family and friends to solve problems and to facilitate action makes it difficult for them to deal with a society and culture in their new homelands in which many traditional functions are handled through public service organizations. Moreover, they did not trust the system which they left behind and will interpret similar symbols as having the same function. For example, uniforms usually worn by officials of the local or central government are to be avoided at all costs. There is a traditional aversion to dealing with the bureaucracy, so they are not only apprehensive about dealing with its representatives but also have little experience with it. Going to court means big trouble. It should be remembered that most countries do not hold the concept of 'innocent until proven guilty' as the basis for their legal systems. It was this way in most of Southeast Asia and, therefore, the attitude of newly arrived refugees is to maintain a low profile as their bottom line. This psychology creates an atmosphere in which success is based on ways to avoid paying taxes, registering in censuses, buying licenses for businesses, and a myriad of other things which seem perfectly normal to citizens in their resettlement areas. This, plus the traditional reliance on family and friends, creates fertile ground for developing a system of favors which can result in bribes and other kinds of payoffs. Taking this all into account, it is not surprising that law enforcement officers often have trouble in dealing with Asians in the new homelands.

4. Adjustment and Culture Shock

The Asian 'newcomers' arrive in a state of cultural shock: they have a hard time with the weather; the water smells bad; the food tastes strange; they can't get freshly butchered meat and fowl; they experience lower gastro-intestinal distress; and they cannot acquire herbal cures that worked for them in Asia. They do not understand the new language and the new culture confuses them. Inability to communicate fosters mutual suspicion which, in turn, reinforces existing stereotypes (on both sides) making it harder to begin the process of acculturation and assimilation.

Many readers have traveled the the Far East with the various military forces. Those who have probably remember that the military bases and posts were models of the home country and that available services and activities went a long way to provide food and other conditions similar to home. While touring around the foreign area, few were forced to live on the economy or give up the material culture which they have come to depend upon in their daily lives. Few visitors become immersed in the culture of the host country. The tourists may have had a deeper immersion, but for a shorter period of time, unless they are "hitchhiking" through exotic parts of the world. In general, most tourists go in groups, stay in hotels with an international standard, and experiment with the local food in very safe places. This group probably has a more realistic feel for what Asian refugees face because they may have had to cope with similar problems but they know that they will, one day, return home.

5. Language

The languages under discussion here are: Chinese, Hmong, (Miao/Meo), Japanese, Korean, Lao, Mien (Yao), Thai, and Vietnamese. Few of the Asian groups read and write languages which are written in a Roman alphabet. All, but Korean and Japanese are tonal. Hmong and Mien are spoken languages which, for all intents and purposes, can be described as having no standardized native writing system. All are so linguistically different than English that native speakers of English take longer to master them than most other languages. By way of comparison, the United States State Department trains its officers in Chinese, Japanese, and Korean for two full years to reach the same level of proficiency it would take the same officers six months to attain in French or Spanish. Not only are the writing systems difficult to deal with, grammatical features and mastery of the sound system; i.e., pronunciation, make learning the spoken language a challenge.

There is a great variety in these writing systems: Tonal vs. non-tonal, character representations, syllabary systems, character and syllabary combinations, alphabets derived from India, and modified Roman alphabets, plus phonetic scripts to represent sounds in languages with no indigenous writing systems of their own.

Chinese is written with a non-alphabetic system of characters where each character has meaning; each character is a word, though the tendency is toward compounds of two or three characters. Characters have little or no phonetic material to indicate pronunciation; pronunciation comes through mimicry, repetition, and memorization.

Historically, China exerted a strong influence over what is present day Korea, Japan, and Vietnam and many cultural features continue to be shared to this day. One example of this is illustrated by language. Both Korean and Japanese use Chinese characters in their writing systems, but not exclusively. Both Japanese and Korean use a syllabary; i.e., symbols which represent syllable sounds in the language. The syllabaries, for Korean and Japanese, were independently created and are not at all the same in appearance so it is easy to tell the difference between the two.

Vietnamese, originally written in Chinese characters, was converted to a Latin/Roman alphabet by a missionary in the 17th Century and officially adopted in the early 1900's. It is written in a modified Roman alphabet which incorporates a system of diacritics to indicate tone, various vowels, and consonants.

Thai and Lao languages are written in alphabets derived from the Devanagari system of Indian origin. Both Hmong (Miao/Meo) and Mien (Yao) originally had no indigenous writing system; however, in recent years phonetic scripts have been devised for each. Both of these phonetic scripts are currently under review and are expected to be accepted as standard sometime in the near future.

6. Tone Languages

Not all languages, which are classified as tone languages, share the same features. For this discussion, a tone language is defined as one in which words have minimal pair pitch level and contour contrasts. A typical and common

English	Chinese	Tone Designation
Mother	Mā	High Level
Hemp	Má	High Rising
Horse	Mǎ	Low Rising
To Scold	Mà	High Falling

Exhibit 1 - Tone Examples

textbook illustration of this feature in Chinese (Standard/Mandarin) is depicted in Exhibit 1.

The Chinese words displayed in Exhibit 1 are represented by a Romanized or Latin alphabet and is not the normal way the Chinese language is written. The diacritics over the vowel are conventional markers to indicate tone in Standard Chinese; an unmarked or neutral tone is also possible.

All Chinese dialects are tonal; each syllable sound may take as many as four tones in Standard Chinese (Mandarin) or as many as seven tones in Cantonese. Vietnamese has six tones in the Northern dialect and five in the Southern dialect. Central or Standard Thai has five tones. Lao has five. Hmong (Miao/Meo) and Mien (Yao) are also tonal while Korean and Japanese are not.

7. Romanized Versions of non-Roman Alphabets

Phonetic transcriptions have been devised to represent sounds in languages which were not written in a Latin alphabet in order to make it possible for English speakers to read and/or to pronounce words in this language. Some of these were simply a rendering of what was believed to be a close approximation in the language of the listener: the person simply wrote down what he or she heard using the English alphabet or French, Dutch, or whatever native language the person wrote. Eventually, this proved to be less accurate because it created as many systems as there were writers. More recently, phonetic transcriptions based on more formal, standardized systems were developed. Yet, even today, there are individuals who attempt to create their own styles without reference to these precisely developed systems. While none of these standard transcriptions can truly record the actual sounds of these languages; it has been expedient to use something and let the experts argue over the pros and cons of each.

Without a standard English spelling for foreign words, few translators can deal properly with foreign place names on English language maps of foreign regions or make references to people in English language materials. Out of this need to standardize English spellings for Asian words, too many 'standards' have been adopted, adapted, revised, and sometimes even based on languages other than English. For example, Chinese may be the most 'Romanized' language of them all: there is Wade-Giles Romanization, Yale Romanization, Pin Yin Romanization (People's Republic of China), National Romanization or Guoyeu Romatzyh (Republic of China), and others created by European scholars and travelers throughout history. This list does not even include those systems which have been devised for other dialects of Chinese.

Similar statements also apply to the other languages under discussion, with the exception of Vietnamese which was standardized and adopted as the national language; it is the only language in the group to adopt a westernized alphabet as its national language. To this date, the phonetic transcriptions or alphabets for Hmong and Mien have yet to be adopted as the national standard for each.

There is another factor which complicates matters. The phonetic transcriptions or Romanized versions of these languages incorporate features which are not always familiar to a majority of English speakers, but are common to language textbooks directed towards speakers of English. To begin with, tones and other phonetic features have to be marked; special consonants and vowels and other diacritics are typed on special typewriters. As a result, many important features of standard phonetic transcriptions are lost when published in English language materials. Therefore, when one reads foreign names in newspapers or reports, what one sees is often second or third generation versions of originals; i.e., the native language was converted to a phonetic script which dealt with all the sound features represented in the original native script and that was 'simplified' to make it easier to deal with in English. The resulting version is pronounced as an English word and, if it appears in print frequently enough, it eventually becomes accepted as English and is incorporated into the lexicon.

Without reference to the original language or the phonetic script which was created to represent the original sounds, the readers have no way of knowing if modified English versions resemble originals to any degree. While the general public should not be too concerned about this, people who come into daily contact with Asians should make an effort to find out just how these names are pronounced or, at least, determine whether or not the Asians with whom they deal have established an accepted version of their names.

Most Asian refugees have accepted non-native pronunciations of their names and some have even changed the spelling to accommodate this. A number of Chinese with the surname, Yang, have changed the spelling to Young, to make things easier. Of course, when this happens investigators know who they are dealing with.

8. Asian Family Names and Personal Names

One of the many things officers discover and find exotic when they come in contact with Asian refugees is that they do not have Western-sounding names. In fact, many names seem impossible to pronounce and, while others look easy enough to pronounce, officers seldom pronounce them correctly. To begin with, there are too many to enumerate; however, there are a number of names which are of high enough frequency to associate them with particular ethnic groups.

9. Family Names

0 Chinese

Wang/Wong, Li/Lee, Lin/Lim/Lam, Chang, Chiang, Huang, Chen Sung,

Soong, Tang, Luk, and so forth. Final stops, -p-, -t-, -k-, indicate a dialect other than standard Chinese or Mandarin. There are also hyphenated surnames like, Ou-Yang and Ssu-Ma.

0   Korean

Kim, Lee/Rhee, Pak/Park, Han/Hahn, Moon/Mun, Choi, Oh, Chun, Paek, Ahn, and others.

0   Japanese

Suzuki, Yamada, Seki, Hashimoto, Kono, etc.

0   Vietnamese

Nguyen, Tran, Phan, Chau, Duong, Ly, Lam, etc.

0   Thai and Lao

The list gets a bit more complicated with Thai and Lao, because law enforcement officers are less familiar or have had less exposure to these names than with other ethnic groups.   Both Thai and Lao family names are distinctly multisyllabic and appear to be very long. Someone has suggested that the longer of the two names is probably the family or surname. For example there are the difficult Thai names of Khanthachawana, Kittikhachon, and Sutthisanronnakon. The Laotian names of Ditthavong, Sananikone, Souvanavong, Sayasithsena can prove to be impossible to work with, as well.

0   Mien (Yao)

Clan names start with the prefix, lub + a designator. However, a generation name functions more like a family name in the Western sense. Generation names are not standardized into a list which is used throughout the culture, they tend to be clan specific, hence, no attempt to list them.

10. Given Names

All the groups have given names but a number do not have middle names. Thai, Lao, Japanese, and Mien (Yao) do not use middle names, though it has been reported that Laotians living in the United States have started to adopt the custom of giving middle names. They are discarding the use of Lao names and are using Christian first and middle names when naming children born outside their native countries.

Generally, Asian male-given names connote positive intellectual qualities, bravery, and skills required by society, etc. Females are given names which connote beautiful or precious things like flowers, moon, rubies, diamonds, orchids, etc. At the risk of oversimplification, it is noted that Japanese male-given names tend to end in 'o' and female given names end in 'ko.' As there is such a greater number of possibilities for given names in these groups, no examples are provided.

11. Childhood names, Nicknames, and Code Names

Many Asians have childhood names which are known by only family and very close friends. They may be as simple as numerical references to order of birth in the family or words like, 'pig' or 'mouse' or some other less complimentary names which are meant to 'fool' the spirits who might take the child away from the family.

The Mien (Yao) have spirit names which are secret and used in rituals and are made public only after death.

8 - 11

Asians have been known to change their names when they change location: change your name - change your luck. Many Chinese who fled the Chinese Mainland in 1929, changed their identity for political reasons. Writers and artists take pseudonyms which convey their new identity, not unlike writers and artists the world over. And, of course, criminals use code names to conceal their real identity or to make known their association with certain groups.

0   Family Names + Given Names

Chinese, Korean, Japanese, and Vietnamese (Vietnamese use Title + Given Name)
Chinese, Korean, and Japanese use Title + Family Name
Hmong (Miao/Meo) conform to the same style as the Chinese.

0   Given Names + Family Names

Thai and Lao (Both use Title + Given Name)

0   Generation Names + Adult Given Names

Mien (Yao) have clan names (similar in function to the Chinese, Korean, and Vietnamese) and adult given names. While the clan name is known, the generation name + the adult given name are the names by which an individual is known. This adult given name is passed as a surname to all children, regardless of sex.

0   Family Names Vs Given Names

One would think that it should be simple enough to learn the original order of occurrence in foreign names, i.e., first, middle, last or last, first, middle and so forth and memorize the system. That would be true enough if officers were dealing within a separate and distinct community of speakers but there are a number of reasons which complicate this, the last of which is caused by adjustments to the American system. This accommodation is seen in telephone book listings, paychecks, driver's licenses, and other documents requiring that all names be uniformly filled out.

Documents may require one sequence while spoken responses require another. The normal order for American names is Given Names (first and middle/ middle initial) + Family Name (family/surname). Therefore, the answer to the question, "What is your name?," is usually given in this order. This sequence is also known as 'The Payroll Signature.' However, there are instances when the family name, followed by the given names are required, as in: 'Jones, Samuel R.' This type of response is commonly heard in the military or in other groups where people are grouped alphabetically by family name. An Asian refugee, not familiar with the system in his new homeland, might conclude that the system is confusing.

0   Scenario

Mr. Nguyen Trung Hieu (Vietnamese) fills out an application for a driver's license. He has been in Canada long enough to know that he should write his name without all the tone marks and other spelling conventions which make the Vietnamese writing system Vietnamese. He also knows that his family name is in the wrong place for Canadians (it is first in the sequence) and that Canadians cannot pronounce it correctly. His given names are Trung Hieu. Trung is a male generational name which his father used to name all of his sons (females do not get generational names). Hieu is his given name and the name by which he is known.

Vietnamese friends and acquaintances refer to him as Hieu. Probably the only time that his family name is used is on documents or as an official signature. If Nguyen Trung Hieu has a rank or title, the sequence will be: Title + Given Name -- not Title + Family Name. From this it can be concluded that the given names in

Vietnamese function like family names in the West in that they combine with the rank or title. 'Mr. Hieu' is the functional equivalent of 'Mr. Jones,' but is more comparable to saying, 'Mr. San.' President Nguyen Cao Ky, was referred to in English as, President Ky, in correct Vietnamese style. When Nguyen Trun Hieu, above, is asked, "What is your name?," he will respond with, "Hieu." If the interviewer asks if that is his last name, Nguyen Trung Hieu may answer affirmatively because he may understand the interviewer to be asking about sequence and not family name.

In all cases, it is preferable to ask the question using Family Name rather than the last name to avoid confusion. If Mr. Nguyen Trung Hieu decides on his own or is forced to write down his name incorrectly on the form, he will carry this mistake with him forever. For example, should he write, Hieu, as his last name and then his first name as Nguyen, followed by Trung. Mr. Hieu will have composed his true name incorrectly even though the three names are close to reality. He should have noted it as: Nguyen, Hieu Trung. The interviewer may address him as Mr. Nguyen (mispronounced), and Mr. Hieu may correct the person by saying, "My name is Hieu. Or Mr. Hieu will just let it pass. One can see the reason for possible confusion and frustration on both sides.

As it would be impossible to list all the names of all of the ethnic groups under discussion here, one way to help identify Asian family names is to become acquainted with those names which are of high frequency in the ethnic groups. Investigating officers should not be reluctant to ask for family names and then to list these family names in their notebooks.

12. Where Do They Come From?

There seems to be an ethnic game played by law enforcement officers in the areas where Asian refugees have settled. That game is: Guess the ethnic origin of a person by their family name. This, of course, leads to stereotyping and stereotyping leads to oversimplification. Many officers begin to think that certain ethnic groups have a 'natural talent' for science, art, or crime. Some people feel that Cantonese are more prone to crime than their Shanghai brothers who are more into banking and other financial dealings. Are the Laos more 'laid back' than the Thais? Are the Koreans more militant than the Japanese? Are the Japanese less creative inventors but better at marketing than other ethnic groups? Many of these statements and others more pejorative are not the sole creation of American observations or prejudice but many are reiterations of statements made by Chinese about Chinese, Thais about Laos, Koreans about Koreans, South Vietnamese about Northern Vietnamese, and the list goes on. One important thing to remember is that Asians cannot be generalized without the investigating officer being open and ready to revise and addend when new information requires it.

13. The Importance of Knowing Ethnic Origin

There is a practical need to know the ethnic origins of the Asians who government must deal with. As stated earlier, there are criminal organizations which are directly related to certain ethnic groups and information relating to ethnic origin can be extremely important to the overall assessments of the type and magnitude of the crime structures in a community.

14. Filing Considerations

A simple filing system, by alphabet, should suffice for most of the languages under discussion. Chinese, however, presents a problem of a different magnitude. Chinese is a non-alphabetic writing system and is tonal, plus the high inventory of homophones (words which sound alike) increases the potential confusion when the characters are represented by a Roman alphabet or script, especially when tone is not marked. This is illustrated by the following examples: there are two surnames;

two distinct characters which can be spelled, Wang, but are pronounced differently because the tones are different. One Wang is pronounced with a High Level tone and the other Wang is pronounced with a High Rising tone. To the Chinese, these two words are as different as the words pig and pit are to English speaking persons. They are written and pronounced differently in Chinese, but, if a Chinese reads Wang as a surname in English, he or she must ask someone which Wang it is.

There are a number of surnames which are contrasted by tone and others have no contrast, except in written, character form. The Chinese do not see these tones and contrasts as problems as long as they are writing and speaking Chinese. In those cases where oral messages cannot be easily communicated or when characters cannot be conveniently used, for instance, in telegraphic communication, the Chinese use a telegraphic code book to deal with this. In English, this code book is called, The Standard Telegraphic Code or STC.

The STC is used much like a dictionary and assigns each character a four- digit number from 0000 to 9999. The four-digit designation for, Wang - High Level Tone, is 3067 and for, Wang - High Rising Tone, is 3769. Occasionally, the surname Huang (STC - 7806) is transcribed Wong by Cantonese speakers. They also transcribe Wang (STC - 3067 and 3769 as Wong. The STC has been adopted by the West to serve a function for which it was not originally designed; categorize characters by numbers for identification, reference, and filing. Furthermore, the STC can be used to assign a number to account for any Romanized version of the same character. As the Romanizations for dialects other than Standard Chinese (Mandarin) have to account for many phonetic features not found in Standard Chinese and which have not been standardized or popularized, speakers of those dialects transcribe their surnames in a less than predictable way.

STC provides the number and the character, plus a Standard Chinese romani- zation or 'pronunciation key' in either Wade-Giles or Pin-Yin, but it will accommodate any romanization the reader wishes to use. Much like Chinese characters themselves, STC is neutral. If, for example, there are three people in files under the name of Wang Fat Choy, the STC book makes it possible for the person who does not read or speak Chinese to specifically identify which name is proper and facilitates filing and referencing. Moreover, by using the STC, one may find there are three different surnames, i.e., 3067, 3769, and 7806 or three different names all filed under the same name with no cross references.

The STC numbers are widely used by government agencies that deal with Chinese place names, personal names, and other material which requires a reference to the original Chinese. The STC provides a system to refer to Chinese characters without learning the language.

15. The Need For Cross-reference

Immigration personnel who check the passports of people entering Hong Kong have an interesting way of handling the problem of name identification. They cross-reference all the names in the passport. They do not assume that the family name is the name under which a person is listed and they treat every name as a possibility. This holds true for non-Asians, as well. As an example is the non-Asian name of Samuel Robert Jones. In this situation, the immigration official always looks under, Jones, then under Samuel, followed by Robert.

Cross-references are important because files may contain earlier or later reports which were entered incorrectly or before more complete information was available. A file user might be led to think there are several and separate cases working, when in reality, there is but one. By developing an extensive bio-data on the person the greater the distinction between individuals can be made.

It takes a great deal of time and effort to learn Asian languages and the behavioral patterns associated with these cultures well enough to carry out an interrogation or debriefing with any degree of accuracy and confidence. Formal interpreting requires a very high level of proficiency in both languages and special interpreter training. Usually there are not enough informal interpreters around and more often than not they are not available on the scene when needed. Furthermore, as most law enforcement officers deal with one or more Asian language groups in a given area, it does not seem likely that there would be sufficient numbers of officers with this kind of background and language proficiency available when needed. In view of the growing magnitude of the Asian crime problem, there appears to be growing argument for instituting a language and cultural training program for those law enforcement officers who have daily contact with Asians. In this way, a pool of informal and reliable interpreters could be developed over a period of years.

Until Departments have sufficient numbers of language-trained staff members, there are a number of considerations and techniques that may be utilized to make the officers' job easier. High among the workable considerations is the establishment of the correct approach or demeanor by the investigating officer. Second, is the locating of the best possible interpreter and reaching an understanding with the interpreter as to his role and the role of the officer.

A good professional interpreter has the confidence of both sides. He or she is well versed in the subject matter in both languages. The interpreter does not participate in the negotiations or the interrogation other than to translate the information that is being passed.

Whether the officer is using formal (a professional interpreter) or informal (an Asian family member or other volunteer) interpreting, the investigating officer should speak directly to the person being addressed, all the while using the first person. The interpreter should also use the first person while performing only as the officer's 'echo' during the two-way exchange. If the officer takes the, 'Find out what he knows about the robbery' approach, he may discover that he has lost control of the situation. The interpreter may take over and go off in directions which are either unnecessary or inappropriate. It is most important to plan the line of questioning carefully before the inquiry begins. This avoids the generalized question, keeps the officer in control of the situation, and allows the respondent sufficient time to answer.

16. The Approach Without an Interpreter

A similar approach is helpful when questioning informants, victims, and suspects who are limited in their use or understanding of English. Work out a questioning format which is simple and direct. Avoid lengthy inquiries. If a specific time must be known and details about a particular weapon, as well, ask the question about the time first and get the full answer before proceeding on with the second and third information needs. Ask questions in a positive manner so that 'yes' and 'no' answers are appropriate and understood. Avoid the negative form of questioning as shown below.

0   "You didn't loan your car to Tram Van Kee, did you?"
0   "You don't have any brothers or sisters living here, right?"

Both negative questions tend to elicit, "Yes, I didn't" or "No, I do" kind of answers.

Try to develop questions which verify earlier information. In other words, build a context for the line of questioning. The one who is asking the questions should always try to speak grammatical English when dealing with Asians, even when the answers testify to a very low proficiency in English. Broken or pidgin English may only serve to confuse. If it is felt that the use of English is not communicating satisfactory, try to find a relative or friend to do some informal interpreting. Younger adults may have better English language skills than more senior types, however, great care should be exercised in choosing the proper assistant. The only informal interpreter available might be the neighborhood gossip whose services would conclude your search for informants.

Whether using an interpreter or not, be careful not to show your temper or become loud. There are some who think that any foreigner will understand English if it is spoken loud enough and in an exasperated tone. Not true. Most Asians feel that people who lose their composure have lost their minds. In Thai, the expression used for calming someone down is roughly equivalent to, 'help regain sanity.' A calm, cool approach is probably much more threatening, especially when the one in authority is being calm and cool.

17. Manner and Approach

Always be professional when dealing with Asians. It is not necessary to emphasize authority; Asians come from very authoritarian cultures and respect, if not fear, officialdom. There is a general reluctance to deal with those in authority and it is no surprise when this trait slows down the process of getting information from either victims or suspects. A more sensitive and patient approach will be more successful when dealing with victims. Suspects should be dealt with using the same procedures as with other, non-Asian suspects.

18. Summary

Stereotyping of different groups of Asians has created a mystique about their culture which tends to confuse and compound the problem of dealing with them as individuals and as a community. As law enforcement officers come to know and understand the Asians in their community, many myths will fall or will be converted into rational observations. It is important not to spend too much time trying to confirm or disprove myths but to be aware of them and let accumulative experience provide the guidance needed.

Traditional approaches for dealing with victims and criminal suspects in all parts of the jurisdiction are equally valid when dealing with crime in the Asian community.

The family is the primary social unit with most Asians. People outside of the family unit are considered to be outsiders and are not quickly trusted. A traditional aversion to dealing with the bureaucracy causes apprehension, if not extreme discomfort. One should not expect Asian refugees to change this attitude just because they are resettled. They do not have nor do they seek out official contacts in the new homelands except in dire emergencies. This is so because many of them found it easier to survive in their native countries by avoiding officials and their bureaucracy whenever possible. If, on the other hand, an investigating officer deals with a victim or offender who once enjoyed high position and rank in Asia, the officer should not expect the victim or offender to show either fear or humbleness, either.

Using the correct pronunciation of foreign words in English is not always the best policy. If one speaks to a victim, witness, or offender who is not used to hearing the foreign pronunciation of the words in the environment of an English sentence, the officer may get only blank stares because of the honest lack of understanding.

When doing debriefings and interrogations with the aid of an informal interpreter, work out a systematic line of questioning. Do not assume the person being questioned has no English understanding or that he or she is totally fluent, either. Use grammatically correct, but simple, direct questions and statements in the native language when debriefing and/or interrogating.

When using a professional interpreter, set the tone as to who is in charge and maintain control of the proceedings. Always be professional in the approach to any problem when dealing with Asians. Nearly all Asians recognize fair and equal treatment and will respond to kind treatment in a positive manner.

Collection Forms, A-1

The three basic forms in this appendix are intended to assist investigators when first making contact with Asians who are thought to possess information relative to a crime or a future crime. Each form has been designed to collect only the most basic of information. On the back side of each form is the Miranda Warning.

1. Purpose

To assist officers in acquiring basic information from witnesses, victims, informants, offenders, arrestees, and suspects when there exists a language barrier and no interpreter is present.

2. Usage

Seek out the family elder, first, before asking for assistance of any kind. Determine if the elder (or family leader) can speak, write, or understand English. If not, then encourage the elder/leader to read and fill out the appropriate language form. If agreeable, have the form filled out in the person's own language for interpretation at a later time. If the person with the desired information is the offender or arrestee, have that person read and initial the Miranda Warning before undertaking the completion of the face of the collection form.

3. Suggestion

Do not add any law enforcement information to the collection form until after the witness, victim, informant, or suspect has completed their writing. This includes the date of the report, and case number at the top of the form, and all information called for at the bottom listed under 'Official Use Only.'

4. Warning

The inclusion of the Miranda Warning is meant to afford the suspect every opportunity to avoid questioning if the suspect so desires. The investigator should be aware, however, that its use does not guarantee the person receiving the warning fully understands its meaning. Every attempt should be made to acquire the services of a reputable and trusted interpreter for providing an in-depth explanation before information collection begins.

5. Publisher's Release

Palmer Enterprises hereby grants full use of the forms in this Appendix for law enforcement use. This release does not extend to any other portion of this book.

INFORMATION FORM

Date of Report _____

Japanese Interview/Interrogation Form

_____ Case Number

| 1. Last Name 氏 | First Name 名 | Middle Name 頭文字 | |

| 2. Home Address 住 所 | | 3. Telephone 電話番号 | |

| 4. Business Address 業務先 | | 5. Telephone 電話番号 | |

| 6. Date of Birth 生年月日 | | 7. Place of Birth 出生地 | |

| 8. Race 人種 | 9. Sex 性別 | 10. Height 背丈 | 11. Weight 重量 | 12. Hair 髪の色 | 13. Eyes 目の色 |

| 14. Immigration I.D. Number 外人登録番号 | | 15. Immigration Status/Dates 外人登録年月日 | |

16. What Do You Wish To Say?
何を言いたいですか。

Use Additional Sheets

17. What Did You See, Hear, Feel?
何を見、聞き、感じましたか。

Use Additional Sheets

18. Who Committed The Crime?
だれの業 (ワザ) ですか。

Use Additional Sheets

OFFICIAL USE ONLY

19. Check One:	20. Reliability Validity	21. Follow-up Recommended:	22. Reporting Officer and Date
Witness ( )	A 1		
Victim ( )	B 2		
Suspect ( )	C 3		
Other ( )	D 4		

Appendix 1, page 3

Palmer design - 1988

Japanese

MIRANDA WARNING

1 You have the absolute right to remain silent.
あなたは法律の絶対権によつて終始沈黙を守ることが出来ます。

2 Anything you say can and will be used against you in a court of law.
あなたの発言は法廷において適用される事ができます。

3 You have the right to consult with an attorney, to be represented by an attorney, and to have an
あなたは法律の権限により、 あなたの弁護士と相談し、 あなたを代押し、

attorney present both before and during any questioning.
迅問（質問）の前後を通じて、 あなたと立合の上、 弁護される事ができます。

4 If you cannot afford to hire an attorney, one will be appointed by the court, free of charge, to represent
若し、 あなたが弁護士を雇うお金が無く、 希望であれば、 迅問の時前に

you before questioning, if you wish.
法廷が弁護士を無料で選定して、 弁護する事ができます。

WAIVER

1 Do you understand each of these rights I have explained to you?
あなたは 私が説明した事が解（わか）りましたか。

2 Having these rights in mind, do you wish to talk with me now?
それでは、 あなたに与えられた権限を頭に入れて、 私の質問に答えて下さい。

| Officer Signature and Date | _____ | Contributor Initials and Date | _____ |

Palmer Design - 1988

Appendix 1, page 4

INFORMATION FORM
Vietnamese Interview/Interrogation Form

Date of Report _____   _____ Case Number

1. Last Name	First Name	Middle Name	
HỌ	TÊN	CHỮ LÓT	

2. Home Address		3. Telephone
ĐỊA CHỈ		SỐ ĐIỆN THOẠI

4. Business Address		5. Telephone
ĐỊA CHỈ NỜI LÀM VIỆC		SỐ ĐIỆN THOẠI

6. Date of Birth		7. Place of Birth	
NGÀY SINH		NỜI SINH	

8. Race	9. Sex	10. Height	11. Weight	12. Hair	13. Eyes
GIỐNG DÂN	NAM/NỮ	CHIỀU CAO	NẶNG	TÓC MÀU	MẮT MÀU

14. Immigration I.D. Number	15. Immigration Status/Dates	
SỐ THẺ XANH, HOẶC SỐ I-94	TÌNH TRẠNG CƯ TRÚ	

16. What Do You Wish To Say?
ÔNG/BÀ MUỐN KHAI BÁO ĐIỀU GÌ ?

_____

_____

Use Additional Sheets

17. What Did You See, Hear, Feel?
ÔNG/BÀ ĐÃ NGHE, THẤY, HOẶC CẢM THẤY ĐIỀU GÌ ?

_____

_____

Use Additional Sheets

18. Who Committed The Crime?
AI LÀ NGƯỜI GÂY RA TỘI ÁC ? (NGƯỜI NÀO DÃ CÓ HÀNH ĐỘNG VI PHẠM LUẬT PHÁP ?)

_____

OFFICIAL USE ONLY   Use Additional Sheets

19. Check One:	20. Reliability Validity	21. Followup Recommended:	22. Reporting Officer and Date
Witness ( )	A 1	_____	
Victim ( )	B 2		
Suspect ( )	C 3	_____	_____
Other ( )	D 4		

Appendix 1, page 5

Vietnamese

MIRANDA WARNING

1 You have the absolute right to remain silent.
BẠN CÓ QUYỀN TUYỆT ĐỐI TRONG VIỆC GIỮ IM LẶNG (KHÔNG KHAI ĐIỀU GÌ CẢ).

2 Anything you say can and will be used against you in a court of law.
NHỮNG ĐIỀU BẠN KHAI CÓ THỂ, VÀ SẼ, ĐƯỢC DÙNG ĐỂ TRUY TỐ BẠN TRƯỚC TÒA .

3 You have the right to consult with an attorney, to be represented by an attorney, and to have an
BẠN CÓ QUYỀN THẢO LUẬN VỚI LUẬT SƯ, NHỜ LUẬT SƯ BIỆN HỘ CHO MÌNH, VÀ YÊU CẦU CÓ

attorney present both before and during any questioning.
SỰ HIỆN DIỆN CỦA LUẬT SƯ TRƯỚC LÚC HAY NGÀY BỊ THẨM VẤN.

4 If you cannot afford to hire an attorney, one will be appointed by the court, free of charge, to represent
NẾU BẠN KHÔNG CÓ TIỀN MƯỚN LUẬT SƯ, VÀ NẾU BẠN YÊU CẦU, TÒA SẼ CHỈ ĐỊNH LUẬT SỬ

you before questioning, if you wish.
MIỄN PHÍ ĐẠI DIỆN CHO BẠN TRƯỚC KHI ĐƯỢC THẨM VẤN.

WAIVER

1 Do you understand each of these rights I have explained to you?
BẠN CÓ HIỂU TỪNG QUYỀN LỢI MÀ TÔI ĐÃ GIẢI THÍCH CHO BẠN KHÔNG ?

2 Having these rights in mind, do you wish to talk with me now?   BIẾT VỀ NHỮNG QUYỀN LỢI VỪA NÓI,
BÂY GIỜ BẠN CÓ MUỐN TRÌNH BÀY SỰ VIỆC CHO TÔI NGHE HAY KHÔNG ?

Officer Signature and Date	_____	Contributor Initials and Date	_____

Palmer Design - 1988

Appendix 1, page 6

INFORMATION FORM

Date of Report _____   Chinese Interview/Interrogation Form   _____ Case Number

1. Last Name 姓 **First Name** 名	

2. Home Address 住宅地址		**3. Telephone** 電話
4. Business Address 辦公地址		**5. Telephone** 電話

6. Date of Birth 出生日期		**7. Place of Birth** 出生地點

8. Race 人種	**9. Sex** 性別	**10. Height** 身高	**11. Weight** 體重	**12. Hair** 頭髮	**13. Eyes** 眼

14. Immigration I.D. Number 移民身份證號碼	**15. Immigration Status/Dates** 移民身份狀況／日期

16. What Do You Wish To Say?
您想講些什麼？

Use Additional Sheets

17. What Did You See, Hear, Feel?
您看到什麼，聽到什麼，感到什麼？

Use Additional Sheets

18. Who Committed The Crime?
誰承認犯罪？

Use Additional Sheets

OFFICIAL USE ONLY

19. Check One:	20. Reliability Validity	21. Followup Recommended:	22. Reporting Officer and Date
Witness ( )	A 1		
Victim ( )	B 2		
Suspect ( )	C 3		
Other ( )	D 4		

Appendix 1, page 7   Palmer Design - 1988

Chinese

MIRANDA WARNING

1	You have the absolute right to remain silent. 您有權利不說話 (不供任何供詞)
2	Anything you say can and will be used against you in a court of law. 任何您所講的話，可以或將會在法庭上用來追控您。
3	You have the right to consult with an attorney, to be represented by an attorney, and to have an 您有權利要求與律師諮詢、相量由律師代辯護，在被審時或審前
	attorney present both before and during any questioning. 都可要求有自己的律師在場。
4	If you cannot afford to hire an attorney, one will be appointed by the court, free of charge, to represent 如果您負担不起律師費，但又想要有律師代為辯護，法庭將免費
	you before questioning, if you wish. 提供律師給您。

WAIVER

1	Do you understand each of these rights I have explained to you? 您是否清楚我所解釋，您自己的權利。
2	Having these rights in mind, do you wish to talk with me now? 您已了解自己的權利後，是否有什麼向我講嗎？

Officer Signature and Date	_____	Contributor Initials and Date	_____

Palmer Design - 1988

Appendix 1, page 8

Immigration Admissions, A-2

Country of Birth	Years of Admissions to United States[1]				Totals
	1965-69	1970-74	1975-79	1980-84	Totals
Vietnam	2,564	14,661	122,987	246,463	386,675
China	65,712	81,202	107,762	129,700	384,376
Cambodia	75	188	5,459	58,694	64,416
Laos	56	196	8,430	102,244	110,926
Japan	18,469	24,301	21,993	16,067	80,830
Korea	18,469	93,445	155,505	163,088	430,507
Totals	105,345	213,993	422,136	716,256	1,457,730
Percents	7	15	29	49	100

1 - Statistical Analysis Branch, U.S. Immigration and Naturalization Service

Immigration   Settlement, A-3

Southeast Asian Refugees - Cumulative State Populations[1]

1984

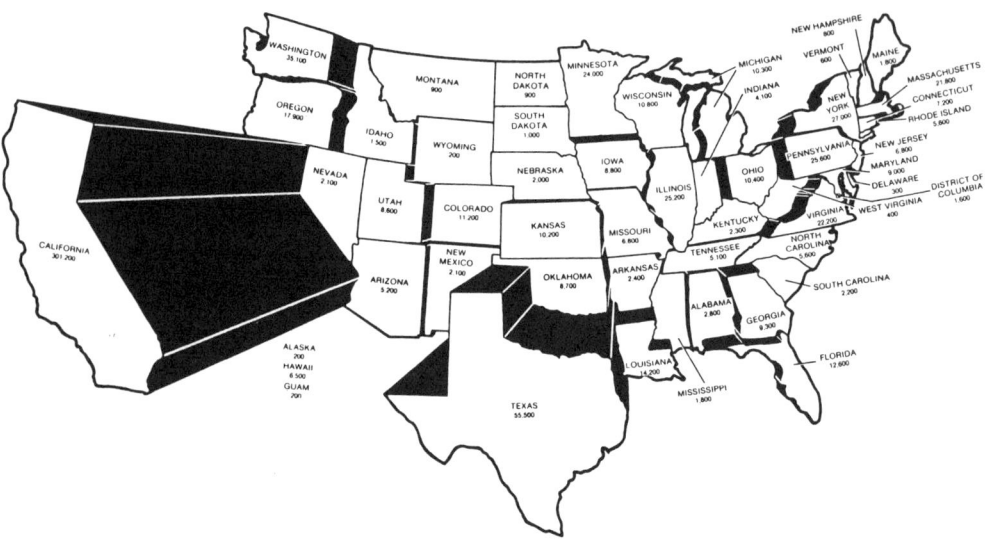

The states listed below are believed to have 20,000 or more Southeast Asian Refugees.   The figures displayed below have been rounded to the nearest 1,000.

0	California	301,000	0	Illinois	25,000
0	Texas	55,000	0	Minnesota	24,000
0	Washington	35,000	0	Massachusetts	22,000
0	New York	27,000	0	Virginia	22,000
0	Pennsylvania	26,000			

---

1 - Office of Refugee Resettlement, U.S. Department of Health and Human Resources

Appendix 3, page 1

Bibliography, A-4

Arnold, William, China Gate, New York, Ballantine Books, 1983.

Bresler, Fenton, The Chinese Mafia, New York, Stein and Day, 1981.

Burns, P.F., Sold Into Slavery, Woman's World, October, 1987.

Buttinger, Joseph, Vietnam: A Political Story, New York, Praeger Publishers, 1972.

Cleveland, Harold Irwin, Massacres of Christians by Heathen Chinese and Horrors of the Boxers, New Haven, Connecticut, Butler and Alger, 1900.

Covell, Alan Carter, Ecstasy, Shamanism in Korea, New Jersey, 1983.

Covell, Dr. Jon Carter, Korea's Cultural Roots, Utah, Moth House Publications, 1981.

Coye, Molly Joel, Editor, China, Yesterday and Today, New York, Bantam Books, 1984.

Daley, Robert, Year of the Dragon, New York, Simon and Schuster, 1981.

Fairbank, Reischauer Craig, East Asia, Tradition and Transformation, Boston, Houghton Mifflin Company, 1978.

Kaplan, David E., Dubro, Alec, Yakuza: The Explosive Account of Japan's Criminal Underworld, Reading, Massachusetts, Addison-Wesley Publishers, 1986.

McCoy, Alfred, <u>The Politics of Heroin in Southeast Asia</u>, New York, Harper and Rowe, 1972.

McCune, Shannon, <u>Korea, Land of Broken Calm</u>, New York, D. Van Nostrand Co., 1966.

Morgan, W.P., <u>Triad Societies in Hong Kong</u>, Hong Kong Government Printer, 1982.

Morris, Jack, <u>Police Informant Management</u>, Palmer Enterprises, Orangevale, California, 1983.

Naylor, R.T., <u>Hot Money and the Politics of Debt</u>, New York, Simon and Schuster, 1987.

Newsweek Magazine, <u>The Gangs of Asia</u>, April, 1985.

Seagrave, Sterling, <u>The Soong Dynasty</u>, New York, Harper and Row, 1985.

Seper, Jerry, <u>Asian Crime in America</u>, Washington Times Newspaper, January, 1986.

Stutman, Robert, <u>Testimony</u>, Permanent Subcommittee on Emerging Criminal Groups, September, 1986.

Victoria Police Force, <u>A Profile of Vietnamese Gang Activity in Victoria</u>, Government Printer, Australia, 1982-86.

Washington Post Newspaper, <u>Drugs are Major Industry in Thailand, Laos, and Burma</u>, March, 1987.

U.S. Government Report, <u>Report on Asian Crime</u>, U.S. Department of Justice, Criminal Division, Office of Police and Management Analysis, February, 1988.

U.S. Government Report, <u>The Nature of Terrorism</u>, Vice President's Task Force, February, 1986.

U.S. Government Report, <u>Organized Crime of Asian Origin, Record of Hearing III</u>, President's Commission on Organized Crime, October, 1984.

Author's Resume, A-5

James R. Badey is a 20 year veteran police officer. He served 9 years as a uniform patrolman, 3 years in narcotics and vice, 3 years in burglary investigations, and since 1983, has worked solely in Arlington, Virginia's Asian community. His work has been multi-faceted in that he simultaneously functions as the Arlington County Police Department's Criminal Intelligence Specialist and Resource and Liaison Officer, as well.

Jim's introduction to the Vietnamese people came in 1965 when, as a Marine Sergeant, he served in Danang, Republic of Vietnam, with the Ninth Marine Expeditionary Brigade. It was during this period in Danang that he met two little war orphans in the Sacred Heart Orphanage, adopted them as his own children, and began making arrangements to bring them to the United States. He was the only member of his Brigade to have his dependents at his side when he left Southeast Asia.

Jim earned his Bachelor of Science degree in 1976 from American University. He has studied Asian history at George Mason University and undertook the study of the Vietnamese language.

As a specialist in Asian crime, Author Jim Badey has testified before the President's Commission on Organized Crime and twice before different U.S. Senate hearings. He is busy giving presentations to law enforcement groups and conferences and providing recruit training on the subject of Asian awareness. He has lectured at the Northern Virginia Community College and at an Asian crime conference in San Francisco.

Now, with his writing of DRAGONS and TIGERS behind him, Author Badey has returned to his original project, the writing of a novel involving his many police experiences in the American-Vietnamese community.